Social-Emotional Learning Through STEAM Projects, Grades 4–5

Social-Emotional Learning Through STEAM Projects, Grades 4–5 helps educators target the development of social and emotional learning (SEL) competencies for high-ability learners through interdisciplinary, project-based inquiry. Aligned with STEAM content standards, each of the nine projects introduces students to a real-world problem through essential questions and the presentation of a primary source document. Both the content and the inquiry process support SEL competency development, from self-awareness to self-management, social awareness, relationship skills, and responsible decision-making. As students work to understand and pose solutions to each problem, they gain the knowledge and practical skills needed to become more socially and emotionally competent individuals in their classroom communities.

Season Mussey has 20 years' experience as a professional educator. She believes that empowering teachers will improve schools, bring hope to families, and transform communities. She has a BA in Biology, an MA in curriculum design and an EdD in teaching and learning.

Social-Emotional Learning Through STEAM Projects, Grades 4–5

Season Mussey

Routledge
Taylor & Francis Group
NEW YORK AND LONDON

Cover image: © Getty Images

First published 2022
by Routledge
605 Third Avenue, New York, NY 10158

and by Routledge
2 Park Square, Milton Park, Abingdon, Oxon, OX14 4RN

Routledge is an imprint of the Taylor & Francis Group, an informa business

© 2022 Taylor & Francis

The right of Season Mussey to be identified as author of this work has been asserted in accordance with sections 77 and 78 of the Copyright, Designs and Patents Act 1988.

All rights reserved. The purchase of this copyright material confers the right on the purchasing institution to photocopy pages which bear the copyright line at the bottom of the page. No other parts of this book may be reprinted or reproduced or utilised in any form or by any electronic, mechanical, or other means, now known or hereafter invented, including photocopying and recording, or in any information storage or retrieval system, without permission in writing from the publishers.

Trademark notice: Product or corporate names may be trademarks or registered trademarks, and are used only for identification and explanation without intent to infringe.

Library of Congress Cataloging-in-Publication Data
A catalog record for this title has been requested

ISBN: 978-1-032-16192-1 (hbk)
ISBN: 978-1-032-16191-4 (pbk)
ISBN: 978-1-003-24744-9 (ebk)

DOI: 10.4324/9781003247449

Typeset in Palatino
by Deanta Global Publishing Services, Chennai, India

To my parents
who taught me to leave a place better than you found it
and
to Max

Contents

1 Teachers' Guide to Social-Emotional Learning through STEAM Projects 1
  Introduction to the Projects 1
  Purpose of the Projects 1
  Overview of the Project Design 2
  Introduction to the 5-E Model of Inquiry 2
  Rationale for Integrating STEAM Projects and SEL 7
  Rationale for Problem-Based Learning 8
  Big Picture Rationale 10
  Guidelines for Successful Implementation of the Projects 11
  Bibliography 12

2 Humans and the Environment 14
  Introduction 14
  Overview of Projects #1, #2, and #3 14
  Project #1: Flooding 15
  Stages of Inquiry 17
  Visualizing a Storm Surge: Build a Model 20
  Extension Activities 25
  Conclusion 27
  Project #2: Climate Change and Communication 27
  Stages of Inquiry 28
  Class Discussion 37
  Project #3: Food Insecurity 38
  Stages of Inquiry 40
  Note 49
  Bibliography 49

3 Humans and Health 52
  Introduction 52
  Overview of Projects #4, #5, and #6 52
  Project #4: In Quarantine: Case Studies of Resilience and Motivation 53
  Stages of Inquiry 55
  Project #5: Peace and Human Health 63
  Stages of Inquiry 64
  Project #6: Healing and Art 72
  Stages of Inquiry 74
  Bibliography 78

4 Technology and Society 81
Introduction 81
An Overview of Projects #7, #8, and #9 82
Project #7: The Polio Vaccine 82
Stages of Inquiry 84
Project #8: Is YouTube Good For Me? 94
Stages of Inquiry 95
Project #9: Technology for Adventures 101
Stages of Inquiry 101
Bibliography 106

Teachers' Guide to Social-Emotional Learning through STEAM Projects

Introduction to the Projects

Social-emotional learning (SEL) through STEAM projects is a series of nine learning experiences designed as projects that can be used as a supplement to classroom science, technology, engineering, art, and mathematics (STEAM) instruction. Each learning experience is related to a real-world issue or problem in one of the following three categories: (1) the environment, (2) humans and health, (3) technology and society (see Figure 1.1). To understand and address the complex issues presented, students will need to develop both academic knowledge and social-emotional competencies.

Purpose of the Projects

Learning in both academic and affective domains is the purpose of the selection and implementation of the nine projects. Teachers will guide students through specific inquiry processes to help them engage with each issue in a relatable context. Students will begin to understand their role in finding applicable solutions to real world problems. The nature of the problems selected, as well as the processes for learning, allow students to develop content knowledge, practice critical and creative thinking, and situate themselves in the world as potential agents of social and environmental change. They will have opportunities to work both independently and in collaborative settings. They will reflect on what they have learned and how they feel about their role in finding solutions to the global problems that they will inherit. They will dialogue with peers and adults about the complexities and outcomes of recent and historical events on our planet. Through participation in and completion of each learning experience, students will grow in the following core areas of social-emotional learning as determined by the Collaborative for Academic, Social, and Emotional Learning (CASEL) (2017): (1) self-awareness, (2) social awareness, (3) self-management, (4) responsible decision-making, and (5) relationship skills.

DOI: 10.4324/9781003247449-1

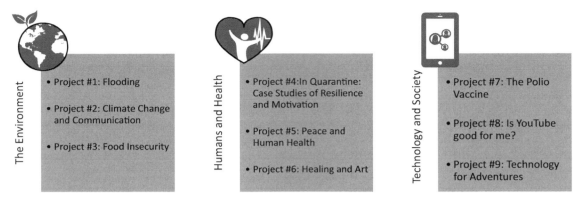

Figure 1.1 Overview of the Nine Projects.

Overview of the Project Design

Using problem-based learning as the pedagogical foundation, students are engaged in each individual project through the introduction of a real-world issue through text. Following the introductory text, students explore one or more primary source documents such as interviews, poems, scientific articles, or other media. The introductory text and primary source documents were strategically included to engage students, tap into their prior knowledge, and put the issue into a relatable context. As students begin to understand the scope of each project, they are invited to engage in dialogues about each problem, exploring possible solutions. They will begin to understand each real-world issue from multiple perspectives. Framed by essential questions, each project is aligned with content standards and SEL competencies appropriate for 4th–5th-grade students.

Introduction to the 5-E Model of Inquiry

During each problem-based learning (PBL) project, students will be guided through stages of inquiry using the 5-E instructional model (Duran & Duran, 2004). In this model, they will be given multiple opportunities to demonstrate their learning. The 5-E model is useful for differentiating instruction, and therefore, teachers will be able to offer multiple modes and opportunities for instruction and assessment for all students based on individual needs. In the 5-E model, students engage, explore, explain, elaborate, and evaluate the real-world issue and their learning. This model allows for attention to the product and the processes of learning.

The 5-E model was traditionally developed for the study of biological sciences (Bybee et al., 2006). It has since been adapted across multiple disciplines and used across the curriculum to deepen student understanding of interdisciplinary concepts, and improve critical thinking (Bennet, 2021). Use of the 5-E model of inquiry can also increase academic achievement, improve attitudes towards learning, and improve scientific processing skills (Cakir, 2017).

In this text, the 5-E model will be used by teachers to guide students through a process of discovery as they seek to understand the issue presented and formulate their own ideas and answers to the essential questions presented.

Stages of Inquiry – The 5 Es: Engage, Explore, Explain, Elaborate, Evaluate

For each project, students will have an opportunity to learn through five stages of inquiry. Each stage has a focus word that begins with the letter E: engage, explore, explain, elaborate, evaluate.

In each stage, students will use critical thinking to complete activities that are aligned with the academic learning outcomes, the social-emotional learning competencies, or both.

Engage

Initially, through reading comprehension of an introductory text, students will engage with the content. During the engage phase of instruction, teachers are working actively to elicit students' preconceived notions and misconceptions about the problem. Teachers will also work to assess students' current levels of knowledge and understanding about the concepts. Simultaneously, the students should be given an opportunity to assess their own levels of content-related knowledge and the SEL competencies targeted for growth. The pre-assessments can be made by posing the project's essential questions before instruction begins.

Explore

During the explore phase of the project, students will investigate a primary source document related to the problem. Using critical thinking, they will analyze the source and draw some initial conclusions. They will explore the concepts further by completing activities independently or in small groups. During this phase, students may decide that they need to conduct more research in order to fully understand what they are learning.

Explain

Upon completion of the exploration phase of the project, students will explain what they have learned thus far. This stage will include an application of knowledge, skills, attitudes, and behaviors. This phase of the project will usually include practice with oral or written communication. Teachers can facilitate learning during this phase by revisiting the essential questions. This is also an opportunity for the teacher to clarify, answer questions, and correct any misconceptions gained during the initial stages of learning.

Elaborate

Next, they will go deeper, elaborating on what they have learned through a creative, hands-on activity, writing assignments, or thought-provoking dialogue. In this phase, there will be a suggestion for a culminating product, where the students may take the multiple examples that they have studied and begin to develop some generalization or applicable conclusions based on what they have learned.

Evaluate

Finally, they will evaluate their learning through written reflection and assessment. The evaluate stage is an important stage for self-awareness and metacognition. Revisit the essential questions one final time. This stage is also the teacher's opportunity to administer any summative assessments in the form of observations, rubrics, written assignments, or exams.

For each stage of inquiry, students may experience multiple learning opportunities through a myriad of activities such as reading, research, writing, small group discussions, presentations, classroom dialogues, reflections, model-building, self-assessments, etc. At each stage of learning, based on individual student learning needs, the classroom teacher can assess, supplement, omit, repeat, and/or change any of the suggested tasks.

> **A Note to Teachers:** You are the expert when it comes to assessing your students' needs and selecting and implementing instructional activities that will engage and inspire them! In each project, you will find multiple opportunities for learning and suggested learning activities. Feel free to use each project design exactly as it is presented or as a supplement to the awesome things you are already doing to promote academic learning, critical and creative thinking, and SEL development in your classroom. If everything in the project will work, use it all! If not, pick and choose what will work for your students this year. I trust you to do what it best for the kids in your classroom.

Expected Learning Results

During each of the nine projects, students are encouraged to engage in their own research and scientific inquiry as a journey toward solutions to the problem and answers to the essential questions. Along the way, through various activities, students are invited to dialogue with peers, adults, experts in the field, and others, as well as to look inward with self-reflective journal prompts.

Due to the complex nature of the problems, students have will have multiple opportunities to engage with and learn content and processes related to STEAM disciplines. For each of the projects, there are expected academic outcomes for learning domain specific vocabulary as well as opportunities to practice reading comprehension and writing processes.

Example of Academic Learning Outcomes from Project #1: Flooding

For example, in Chapter 2, Project #1 students dive into the topic of flooding. During this project, they will learn new vocabulary related to flooding such as the term: storm surge.

They will also build a model demonstrating the impacts of storm surge and the resulting waves on a coastal community. In this experience, they are meeting science and engineering performance expectations for the Next Generation Science Standards for 4th- and 5th-grade science (National Research Council, 2013). Beyond that, when students read multiple texts and then write about the potential impact of flooding on a community, they will be developing some of the specific reading and writing skills outlined in the English Language Arts common core standards for 4th and 5th grade (National Governors Association Center for Best Practices, Council of Chief State School Officers, 2010). Specifically, they will be reading informational texts and learning how to integrate ideas from multiple sources to write or speak knowledgeably. They will be writing their own informational texts using facts and evidence to convey a message clearly. For each project, targeted academic standards will be identified.

Example of Social-Emotional Learning Outcomes from Project #1: Flooding

Beyond supporting academic development including knowledge and skills in STEAM disciplines, these projects serve to support students as they develop specific social-emotional learning (SEL) competencies. Each project will target specific SEL competencies, as outlined in the CASEL (2017) framework. These competencies may fall under one or more of the following core areas: self-awareness, self-management, social awareness, relationships, and responsible decision-making.

For example, in Project #1 – flooding – students will read poems written by 4th–5th-graders who have lived through the devastating effects of flooding; they will begin to develop social awareness as they empathize with the student poets. They will practice exhibiting compassion for others who are experiencing the loss or grief that can accompany weather-related environmental changes. In addition, they will consider their own family's level of preparedness for weather-related flooding, and work with their families to develop a safety plan. This helps students gain a sense of purpose (self-awareness) as well as skills for self-management and relationship building through effectively communicating the need for safety during times of weather-related flooding. Project #1 is one example of the interdisciplinary nature of the projects in this collection and the diversity of expected learning outcomes. For each project, targeted SEL competencies will be identified.

Other Outcomes – Mindfulness in the Classroom

Each project presented in this book will challenge teachers and students to process difficult issues. The essential questions provoke thought and emotional responses. Finding solutions to the complicated problems will require critical thinking, creative thinking, and mindfulness.

Jon Kabat-Zinn (2003, p. 145) describes mindfulness as "the awareness that emerges through paying attention on purpose, in the present moment, and nonjudgmentally to the unfolding of experience moment by moment." Consider how each project might help you guide your students on a journey toward using mindfulness principles and practices in the classroom.

Mindfulness can help students develop many desirable social-emotional competencies (Mussey, 2019). For example, mindful individuals, often more self- and socially aware, can identify their own strengths as well as the strengths of others. They work hard to problem-solve and find connections to others as they contribute on teams. Mindful individuals can often better regulate their emotions and find success through goal setting and taking the initiative. As a classroom teacher, you can help students practice mindfulness as an avenue toward SEL competence. Using mindfulness in the classroom is a way to improve overall teacher effectiveness, increase student learning, and even remind you of the joys of teaching and learning (Mussey, 2019). Here are three mindfulness principles that you can use as you guide students through the projects.

Cultivate Connections

As students engage in each project, encourage them to find connections between themselves, the topics, and one another. For example, what is their role in addressing each issue? What can they do? How can they help one another? One effective strategy for cultivating connections is to facilitate collaboration. Another is through effective questioning strategies. Refer to the essential questions before, during, and after the completion of each project activity. Cultivating connections promotes patience, compassion, empathy, and humility amongst students and their peers.

Practice Gratitude

Help students practice gratitude as they complete the projects. This might include helping them find gratitude for the difficult work that they are doing. You may consider encouraging them to thank their peers often for the help that they get from one another during groupwork. You may also consider helping them to show or feel gratitude for some of the individuals who they will meet through analysis of the primary source documents throughout the book. Gratitude improves the strength of relationships (Algoe, 2012).

Breathe and Move

Allow students to breathe and move before, during, and after some of the activities and experiences in the projects. For example, take breathing breaks when necessary. Pause and take three breaths, inhaling and exhaling deeply. Count for the students as they breathe in for three seconds and out for four. Conscious breathing improves mental functions (Goldman, 2017). Move between tasks. Go for short walks outside, if possible. As they are processing some of the difficult issues, students and teachers alike may benefit from incorporating intentional breathing and movement into lesson plans. Consider scheduling breathing and movement activities before or after difficult tasks, as they often allow time and space for reflection.

> **A Note to Teachers:** Since the projects aim to help students think about their personal and collective role in the global issues that will affect their lives in the future, mindfulness is essential. Mindfulness matters. Try it!

Rationale for Integrating STEAM Projects and SEL

Time is one of the greatest and most limited resources for the classroom teacher and 21st-century learner. Pressure and demands from our modern, standards-based curricula and testing-based culture may prove to discourage the classroom teacher from designing projects that allow students to use their creative minds for problem-solving. Problem-solving takes time. When teachers use inquiry-based approaches to instruction and pose problems with open-ended questions, they must give students enough time to answer them. Giving time is an investment in the development of students' critical thinking skills. The payoff is worth the investment. This time-intensive, problem-solving practice is the work that all students, especially high-achieving students, need. But, how can teachers negotiate the use of the limited resource of time? How can they balance the expectations of ensuring rigorous academic learning, while simultaneously allowing opportunities to work together to develop life skills and the social-emotional competencies that they will need to thrive as a contributing member of society? Without the implementation of strategic, interdisciplinary learning experiences, it is nearly impossible for the classroom teacher to do all that is required to teach the whole child. Teachers need resources that support interdisciplinary learning objectives across multiple domains.

This book was written with that need in mind. The projects within the chapters that follow will help teachers as they help students develop their intellectual and leadership potential. Through learning experiences that address cognitive and affective learning domains, and grade-appropriate academic standards, this resource was developed as a support to teachers as they navigate the competing demands of the 21st-century classroom.

> **A Note to Teachers:** You are awesome! Use this book to support your diverse learners' needs as you strive to promote equity and excellence in our nation's schools.

Support for Gifted Learners

Social-Emotional Learning Through STEAM Projects will support the needs of gifted learners who typically grasp grade-level standards more quickly. The projects in this book include creative processes of inquiry and challenging opportunities to develop original products and solutions to real-world problems. To solve the selected STEAM issues, social and emotional competence is necessary. Each of the issues identified in this text are complex and multifaceted and will require more than just scientific knowledge and skills. Finding sustainable solutions to these issues will require critical thinking, creative thinking, mindfulness, empathetic thinking, *and* scientific knowledge and skills. Students will become aware of the bigger picture surrounding our global problems. They will begin to see the importance of scientific literacy and cooperation. They will begin to learn how to use their gifts to make positive change. The hope is that gifted learners will be empowered by the opportunity to think about and address these issues now. Students will learn that kids can have a global impact on the future of humanity.

Rationale for Problem-Based Learning

Problem-based learning is a pedagogical approach that uses problems in case studies to achieve the desired learning outcomes (Walsh, 2005). The origins of this teaching methodology date back to the 1960s when a medical school professor, Harold Barrows, began using problem-based learning at McMaster's University (Schmidt, 2012). Barrows, like many educators today, noticed that his students seemed to master concepts and domain-specific knowledge on exams, but had difficulty applying it in real-world settings. Problem-based learning offers students an opportunity to engage in problem-solving exercises, going beyond rote memorization of facts (Barrows, 1986; Barrows, 1998). This higher order thinking is what the Barrows' medical students needed in their clinical practice. Similarly, this higher-order thinking is what humanity needs to solve some of the global issues that challenge our existence. In these cases, it seems that higher-order thinking can be a matter of life or death. Therefore, it seems critical to provide students the opportunity to practice thinking in ways that really can make a difference in our world.

The students in our classrooms today need practice and opportunities to exercise their thinking skills and apply knowledge to problems that they care about. In problem-based learning (PBL), the problems themselves become the motivators for the learning. PBL is student-centered. Given the nature of the STEAM issues that were selected for this book, and given the unique opportunity to support students' development of SEL as integrated objectives in lessons, a problem-based learning approach seems reasonable and justified.

In problem-based learning, students work collaboratively to tackle open-ended questions. For each of the nine projects in this book, essential questions can drive the learning outcomes. Teachers can use the essential questions as both an outline for instruction as well as pre and post assessments for learning.

According to Nilson (2010), in problem-based learning, teachers will plan learning experiences, ensuring opportunities for both individual and collaborative learning. Some other benefits of PBL include developing leadership skills, practicing oral and written language skills, using critical thinking, and making connections between what they discover and grade-level content. In addition, PBL allows for the development and utilization of research skills, problem-solving, and interdisciplinary learning. Furthermore, many of the tenets of PBL support the development of social-emotional learning competencies.

For example, one common expectation of PBL is working in teams. This aligns directly with the SEL competency of practicing teamwork and collaborative problem-solving. Working in teams allows students to develop relationship skills and social awareness while learning how to effectively communicate. Students must learn to consider the varied, multiple perspectives of teammates. See Table 1.1 for some examples of how the skills that students develop during PBL align with desirable SEL learning outcomes.

Table 1.1 Alignment of Skills Developed During PBL with SEL Competencies

Skills Developed During Problem-Based Learning	Related Social-Emotional Learning Competencies
Working in teams	**Social awareness:** Taking others' perspectives, recognizing situational demands, understanding social norms **Relationship skills:** Communicating effectively, developing positive relationship, offering help, resolving conflict
Managing projects and holding leadership roles	**Self-management:** Having the courage to take initiative, setting collective goals **Relationship skills:** Showing leadership in groups
Effective oral and written communication	**Relationship skills:** Communicating effectively
Self-directed learning / working independently	**Self-management:** Using planning and organization skills, setting personal goals, taking initiative
Applying course content to real-world examples	**Responsible decision-making:** Recognizing how critical thinking skills are useful both inside and outside of school, demonstrating curiosity and open-mindedness, identifying solutions for personal and social problems, learning to make a reasoned judgment after analyzing information, data, facts
Self-awareness and evaluation of group process	**Self-awareness:** Integrating personal and social identities, identifying personal, cultural, and linguistic assets, identifying one's emotions
Critical thinking and analysis	**Responsible decision-making:** Recognizing how critical thinking skills are useful both inside and outside of school, learning to make a reasoned judgment after analyzing information, data, facts

A Note to Teachers: There are so many amazing final product ideas that students can use to demonstrate their findings during PBL. Many are included in the nine projects in this book; however, here are a few more. General product ideas: design an APP, write an article for a blog, conduct a science experiment, write a business plan, write a script for a film, present a talk in the style of Ted Talks, make a video for YouTube, create a campaign poster, plan a fundraising event, re-enact a scene from history, perform a dramatic interpretation of a historical figure or event, design a class farm, paint a community mural, design a virtual workshop, lead a discussion on Zoom. As you can see, there are many ways for students to creatively demonstrate their knowledge during PBL.

Big Picture Rationale

Today, more than ever before, we have an opportunity to help students develop the behaviors, skills, and attitudes that will help them succeed in their academic, personal, and professional lives. It is the hope of many educators that we do more than teach reading, writing, and arithmetic. We desire to teach students how to be contributing, positive, empathetic members of their communities. We can show them, both by our own example, and in the stories and examples of others, that it is possible to continue to be a positive source of light and hope. Even as our culture struggles with division, negativity, and biological, environmental, social, and emotional disasters, we can make a positive difference. For many educators, we entered this profession with that ideal in mind. We chose to be teachers so that we could make a difference. But, what does that actually mean in terms of classroom curriculum selection and teaching methodologies?

One Strategy for Making a Difference

One strategy for making a difference is to teach students how to think about and search for solutions to real-world issues. Consider being bold in your selection of problem-based learning topics. Select from issues that have consistently plagued humanity. Choose critical issues related to the environment, climate change, hunger, health, and technology.

Global Problems and Goals

The United Nations has determined 17 global issues that need solutions now (United Nations, 2021). From these, they have published 17 global goals with the hope of finding solutions by the year 2030. Some of the goals include ending poverty, ending hunger, achieving gender equality, taking climate action, and ensuring clean water and sanitation for all humans on earth. See Table 1.2 for a complete list of the United Nations' 17 Goals (UN 17).

How to Change the World

As you can see, these are mammoth-sized issues that exist on our planet. If not addressed, these issues will affect the quality of life for our children and our children's children. It will take cooperation, innovation, and communication to solve these issues. Many of the solutions will come from our nations' youth. So, why not encourage students to start thinking about some of these problems now? If we do, we can be assured that students will learn new academic vocabulary and procedural knowledge, while simultaneously developing critical-thinking skills. They will become more curious, experience self-efficacy, recognize multiple perspectives, develop a sense of identity and consider their role in making a positive difference on earth.

The nine projects selected for this book were inspired by the UN 17 and the motivation to make the world a better place. It is our responsibility to help students develop the scientific

Table 1.2 List of the 17 Global Goals Proposed by the United Nations in 2013

The United Nations' 17 Global Goals
1. No poverty
2. Zero hunger
3. Good health and well-being
4. Quality education
5. Gender equality
6. Clean water and sanitation
7. Affordable and clean energy
8. Decent work and economic growth
9. Industry, innovation, and infrastructure
10. Reduced inequalities
11. Sustainable cities and communities
12. Responsible consumption and production
13. Climate action
14. Life below water
15. Life on land
16. Peace, justice, and strong institutions
17. Partnerships for the goals

Source: United Nations (2021).

literacy and social-emotional competence that they will need to face these issues and more. How wonderful to offer our youth an opportunity to see both the big picture and learn how their individual and collective contributions can change the world.

Guidelines for Successful Implementation of the Projects

The project topics and real-world problems were strategically selected because they are critical, current, and interdisciplinary issues that our younger generation will surely encounter, address, and hopefully solve in their lifetimes. Critical thinking, creative thinking, rigorous academic development of knowledge and skills, and social-emotional competency development are the ultimate goals of these projects. Since the goals are ambitious, here are some tips and tricks for successful implementation of the projects.

Tips and Tricks for Teachers

1. Approach each project and the inquiry-based, instructional model with high expectations for learners. Make your expectations for both processes and products explicit. Be clear and consistent.
2. A mindset of learner-centeredness is essential. Meet each learner where they are and differentiate the activities as needed. Combine your knowledge of pedagogy with what you know about your specific teaching context to craft learning experiences appropriate for each student that you serve. This may mean modifying some of the instructional activities, selecting more challenging assessments, or

finding more accessible text options. Feel free to use your professional expertise to guide those decisions.
3. There will be opportunities for whole-group and direct instruction; however, the nature of much of this project-based, student inquiry is that of independent or small group study. Therefore, prepare to provide some direct instruction and then give students time to learn on their own using the scaffolded activities provided. Release the responsibility to them. Trust your students. Try to remain flexible to the conclusions that they find, prompting them to support their ideas with textual evidence and factual examples. Consider serving the students during these projects in the role of facilitator. Be strategic about the composition of your students' collaborative learning teams. Establish guidelines and expectations for accountability in groups.

Efficacy and Excellence

Through participation in the projects, students will experience efficacy in academic work and identity development work central to social-emotional learning (SEL). It is the hope that this series will challenge students to believe that they can make a difference. Through creative conversations and a commitment to a high standard of excellence, in a community of like-minded thinkers, they will observe that real-world change is possible.

Bibliography

Algoe, S.B. (2012). Find, Remind, and Bind: The Functions of Gratitude in Everyday Relationships. *Social and Personality Psychology Compass*, 6, 455–469. https://doi.org/10.1111/j.1751-9004.2012.00439.x

Barrows, H.S. (1986). A Taxonomy of Problem-based Learning Methods. *Medical Education*, 20, 481–486. https://doi.org/10.1111/j.1365-2923.1986.tb01386.x

Barrows, H.S. (1998). The Essentials of Problem-based Learning. *Journal of Dental Education*, 62(9), 630–633.

Bennett, C. (2021). What Is the 5 E Instructional Model? *ThoughtCo*, Feb. 17, 2021. Retrieved on June 20, 2021 from https://thoughtco.com/5-e-instructional-model-4628150

Bybee, P.W., Taylor, J.A., Gardner, A., Van Scotter, P., Powell, J.C., Westbrook, A., Landes, N. (2006). The BSCS 5E Instructional Model: Origins and Effectiveness. A Report Prepared for the Office of Science Education National Institute of Health. Retrieved on May 30, 2021 from https://media.bscs.org/bscsmw/5es/bscs_5e_full_report.pdf

Cakir, N.K. (2017). Effect of 5E Learning Model on Academic Achievement, Attitude and Science Process Skills: Meta-Analysis Study. *Journal of Education and Training Studies*, [S.l.], 5(11), 157–170, oct. 2017. ISSN 2324-8068. Retrieved on July 26, 2021 from https://redfame.com/journal/index.php/jets/article/view/2649; http://dx.doi.org/10.11114/jets.v5i11.2649

Collaborative for Academic, Social and Emotional Learning. (2017). SEL: What are the Core Competence Areas and There are they Promoted? Retrieved on December 8, 2020 from https://casel.org/sel-framework/

Duran, L.B., & Duran, E. (2004). The 5E Instructional Model: A Learning Cycle Approach for Inquiry-Based Science Teaching. *The Science Education Review*, 3(2), 49–57. Retrieved on July 6, 2021 from https://files.eric.ed.gov/fulltext/EJ1058007.pdf

Goldman, B. (2017). Brain Study Shows How Slow Breathing Induces Tranquility (2017, March 31). Retrieved on 26 July 2021 from https://medicalxpress.com/news/2017-03-brain-tranquility.html

Kabat-Zinn, J. (2003). Mindfulness Based Interventions in Context: Past, Present, and Future. *Clinical Psychology, Science and Practice*, 10, 144–156.

Mussey, S. (2019). *Mindfulness in the Classroom: Mindful Principles for Social and Emotional Learning.* Waco, TX: Prufrock Press.

National Governors Association Center for Best Practices, Council of Chief State School Officers. (2010). *Common Core State Standards.* Washington D.C.: Author. http://corestandards.org/n

National Research Council. (2013). *Next Generation Science Standards: For States, By States.* Washington, DC: The National Academies Press. https://doi.org/10.17226/18290.

Nilson, L.B. (2010). *Teaching At Its Best: A Research-based Resource for College Instructors* (2nd ed.). San Francisco, CA: Jossey-Bass.

Schmidt, H.G. (2012). A Brief History of Problem-based Learning. In: O'Grady, G., Yew, E., Goh, K., Schmidt, H. (eds.) *One-Day, One-Problem.* Singapore: Springer. https://doi.org/10.1007/978-981-4021-75-3_2

United Nations. (2021). THE 17 GOALS. Sustainable Development [webpage]. Retrieved on August 1, 2021 from https://sdgs.un.org/goals

Walsh, A. (2005). *The Tutor in Problem Based Learning: A Novice's Guide.* McMaster University.

Humans and the Environment

Introduction

Chapter 2 includes three projects related to humans and our interaction with the environment. We will consider how the environment can affect us as well as how we can change the environment, for better or worse. Therefore, we are looking at reciprocal relationships. In this chapter, we will consider our natural environment, including the local weather and our global climate. We will also explore the availability of resources in our environments, such as food. We will look at how our social environments can positively affect the distribution of food resources in our communities. We will also explore how we feel about our relationship with the natural and social environment. Each project will include opportunities to gain awareness of how what we do matters and can make a difference in the lives of other humans as well as in the lives of plants and animals with whom we share space on earth. All three projects are aligned with academic standards for 4th–5th graders and core SEL competencies.

Overview of Projects #1, #2, and #3

Weather and climate are non-living factors that influence living organisms in the natural environment. Project #1 is an exploration of how the weather-related issue of flooding can have both positive and negative impacts on communities on the land and on ecosystems offshore. Project #2 goes beyond looking at a single, weather-related event and explores climate and weather patterns over time. In Project #2, we look specifically at climate change and communication. Namely, we will explore the current issue of global warming and begin to understand the importance of caring about how what we do might affect future generations. We meet a student who is passionate about this issue, and who models how to use powerful communication skills to influence others to take climate action. Project #3 is about our social environments and the distribution of food resources in communities. Students learn the terms food insecurity and food desert. During this project, students will discover how the actions of a few passionate individuals can begin to solve the problem of hunger in America. Students will be challenged to explore how creative solutions, such as community gardens, contribute to more equitable distribution of food resources in our local communities (Table 2.1).

DOI: 10.4324/9781003247449-2

Humans and the Environment   15

Table 2.1 Humans and the Environment Projects and Their Alignment to 4th/5th-Grade Academic Standards and SEL Competencies

Projects	Targeted Academic Standards For 4th–5th grade	Targeted SEL Core Competencies
1 – Flooding	Science Standards NGSS[1] 4-ESS3-2, ESS3.C, 5-PS3-1 Common Core Standards English Language Arts CCSS.ELA-Literacy W.4.1, W.4.4, W.5.1, W.5.4	**Self-awareness:** Identify strengths **Social awareness:** Develop empathy **Self-management:** Take initiative **Responsible decision-making:** Anticipate consequences, reflect on one's role
2 – Climate Change and Communication	Science Standards NGSS[1] 4-ESS3-1, 5-ESS2-2 Common Core Standards English Language Arts, Math Problems W4.8, R1.5.7, MP.2,	**Self-awareness:** Develop interests, gain a sense of purpose, explore their role **Responsible decision-making:** Practice open-mindedness, find solutions for social problems **Social awareness:** Recognize strengths in others
3 – Food Insecurity	Common Core Standards Math CCSS.Math.Content.4.OM.2 Reading CCSS.ELA-literacy R1.4.1, R2.4.2 Writing CCSS.ELA-Literacy E.4.3, W.5.3	**Social awareness:** Express concern and compassion for others; identify unjust norms **Responsible decision-making:** Recognize role in community well-being **Self-awareness:** Link feelings, values, and thoughts **Relationship skills:** Seek or offer help when needed

Project #1: Flooding
Academic Learning Objectives

Students will:

a) Make observations and provide evidence of the effects of weathering on environments, including water flow.
b) Construct and analyze models to explain and give evidence of their understandings.

16 Humans and the Environment

c) Generate solutions to minimize the effects of natural processes on humans.
d) Understand that human activities have an impact on the environment and that we are seeking empirical evidence that will help us protect the earth's resources.

SEL Competencies

a) **Social awareness:** When studying the effects of weather-related flooding on human populations, students will develop empathy for those who have lived through catastrophic flooding events. They will gain social awareness as they understand how kids and adults used the written word to process what happened in the form of poetry and scientific studies. They will demonstrate their understanding during small group discussions.
b) **Self-awareness:** Students will practice self-awareness as they think about how the environmental and human impacts of flooding disasters make them feel, identifying their own emotions and thoughts. They will demonstrate this awareness in written reflections.
c) **Responsible decision-making and self-management:** Students will develop skills in responsible decision-making as they think through creating a plan for safety before/during/after flooding. They will practice having the courage to take the initiative and communicate their plan to members of their household.

Essential questions will guide you as you move through the stages of inquiry. Assess yourself on these questions before, during, and after you complete the activities. Work with your teacher to determine which activities and questions you will answer individually and which you will work on in collaborative groups.

Essential Questions

1. What are the immediate and long-lasting consequences of weather-related flooding on environments?
2. What are some positive and negative outcomes of flooding on land and offshore?
3. How can we help people before, during, and after weather-related floods?
4. What are some other ways that we could reduce the effects of flooding on human communities?

A Note to Students: Spend time working through the 5 E model of inquiry as you learn about the problem of flooding. Using this inquiry process, you will engage in the problem, explore the issues, explain some of your findings, elaborate on what you have learned with additional examples, and evaluate your understanding of the issue and your role in finding solutions to real-world problems.

Stages of Inquiry

Introduction to the Problem

On August 25, 2017, Hurricane Harvey, a Category 4 hurricane made landfall on the central Texas Coast near the small town of Rockport, TX. For four days, the storm stalled over the large metropolitan area of Houston, TX. There were many devastating consequences of Hurricane Harvey. Flooding, caused by a significant storm surge, was among the greatest contributor to loss of property and life. Flooding can have devastating impacts on humans and the environment.

After the flooding, the *Houston Chronicle,* an organization called Writer's in Schools (2021), and classroom teachers alike asked students who had experienced the flooding to write poems about their experiences. Some of the poems were curated and placed on exhibit in an online museum: The Houston Flood Museum.

Engage

Visit the Houston Flood Museum online. Go here: https://houstonfloodmuseum.org/

Go to the Hurricane Harvey Exhibit and browse through the collection "The Ocean is Wearing My Clothes": Student Stories and Poems.

Go here: https://houstonfloodmuseum.org/category/hurricane-harvey/the-ocean-is-wearing-my-clothes-student-stories-and-poems/

Read some of the poems and stories and select your favorite. Spend some time thinking about how students must have felt during the 2017 floods. Empathy is the ability to understand the feelings of others. Can you empathize with the students? Respond to the following reflective writing prompts.

Engage Activities

See Figure 2.1.

Explore

Read the poem by Jay, 4th grade (Table 2.2). This poem, entitled "Thief," was reprinted with permission from Writers in the Schools. It was originally published in the Hurricane Harvey Exhibit online in the Houston Flood Museum (2017b). You can find the original poem at the following web address: https://houstonfloodmuseum.org/jay-4th-grade/

18   Humans and the Environment

Name_____

 Read:

In the *aftermath* of Hurricane Harvey, an organization called writers in the schools visited *emergency shelters* where many families from Houston were *temporarily* living. They had to *evacuate* their homes and wait for the flood waters to *recede*. Many children were there too. The writers in the schools' *volunteers* asked the students to write about their experiences. The students became *heroes* in their stories instead of *victims*.

> Key Words:
> *aftermath, emergency shelters, temporarily, evacuate, recede, volunteers, heroes, victims*

Discuss:

In small groups, discuss the meaning of each of the key words. Share your thoughts about how the families living in the emergency shelters during the floods may have felt. Share your favorite poems and stories from the Houston Flood Museum collection.

Write:

1. Write a sentence or two describing how the students may have felt while they were staying in the emergency flood shelters. Do you think that they were afraid? How would you have felt? Do you think that writing about their experiences helped them? How?
2. Identify your favorite poem or story from The Houston Flood Museum Exhibit. Why did you like it? What did you learn from reading this poem or story?
3. How does your visit to the Houston Flood Museum help you empathize with students who have lived through weather-related disasters, such as floods?

Figure 2.1 Project #1, Engage Activities.

Copyright material from Season Mussey (2022),
Social-Emotional Learning Through STEAM Projects, Grades 4–5, Routledge

Table 2.2 A Poem: Thief by Jay, 4th grade (reprinted with permission from Writers in the Schools. Originally displayed in the Houston Flood Museum Hurricane Harvey Collection)

> **Thief by Jay, 4th grade**
> Floods are thieves that made my favorite cow, Cursey, die. During the flood, I was with my mom. My mom was making dinner for everybody. When the news came on, I saw that Port Lavaca was flooding. When the flood was over, I went to see if Cursey was okay, but instead of her being alive, she was dead.
> So I ran inside upset and my grandpa came and said, "What's wrong?"
> I said, "I lost Cursey."
> We went outside to see her. When we were outside, I found Cursey's gold bell on the floor.

Explore Activities

SMALL GROUP DISCUSSION QUESTIONS

1. How did the writer, Jay, feel about the flooding that they experienced?
2. How did the writer, Jay, feel about his cow, Cursey?
3. Have you ever experienced a loss like this because of a weather-related catastrophe or other natural disaster?
4. The title of Jay's poem is "Thief." Why do you think he chose this title? What was stolen? Who is the thief?

> **Explore:** Write your own poem about a time when you felt something was stolen from you.
>   Or,
>   Write a letter to Jay, the author of the poem, "Thief," expressing your feelings about his loss. Empathize with him, and let him know that you have compassion for him and other flood victims. Express your gratitude for the poem that he shared.

Explain: Storm Surge

One of the most devastating impacts of the hurricane was flooding caused by significant storm surge. According to the National Hurricane Center's report on Hurricane Harvey (Blake & Zelinsky, 2018), the flood surge levels reached 6–10 feet above ground level. According to the National Ocean Service (NOAA, 2021), a storm surge is a rise in the sea level due to a storm. The storm surge creates abnormally high tides, usually because of high winds pushing the waves and water to shore. Land that is usually *not* affected by tides would be underwater during a storm surge. Imagine if a storm surge suddenly flooded your community with 6–10 feet of water. The flooding would have devastating effects. In order to better understand and visualize a natural phenomenon, scientists construct models. In this exploration of flooding, you will build a model of a coastal community. Then, you will demonstrate what a 6–10-foot storm surge would do to this community (Figure 2.2).

Humans and the Environment

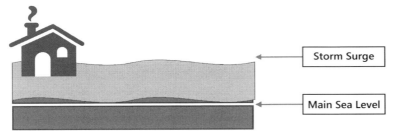

Figure 2.2 Visualizing a Storm Surge: Build a Model.

Visualizing a Storm Surge: Build a Model

Independently, explore the concept of storm surge. Using a shoe box, Legos, modeling clay, small toy animals and plants, or other materials, build a small model of a coastal community. Be sure to indicate the main sea level. Now, demonstrate what will happen to this community during a flood. Flood your model with water, representing a flood surge of 6–10 feet. What buildings become submerged? What plants become submerged? Where can animals and people seek shelter from the waves? Share this demonstration with your small group. Discuss how the coastal community could minimize the devastation of flooding by building certain flood barriers, regulating where homes and schools can be built, and/or developing safety plans for preparation and evacuation in the event of flooding (Figure 2.3).

	Below Expectations (10)	Approaching Expectations (15)	Meets Expectations (20)	Exceeds Expectations (25)	Total (out of 100)
Explains Scientific Concepts	Student does not use scientific terms correctly. Explanation is unclear or off-topic.	Student explains concept of flooding in general but does not use vocabulary accurately. It is unclear if the student understands the concepts.	Student explains some of the concepts related to storm surge and uses some of the vocabulary. Demonstrates the impact that floods have on humans but does not consider animal and plant populations.	Student explains the concepts of storm surge, main sea level, and flooding accurately and completely. Demonstrates understanding of the impact that storm surge can have on human communities, and coastal animal and plant populations.	
Model Relates to Concepts	Model does not relate to real-world issue. No labels are utilized.	It is unclear how the model relates to real-world concepts. Labels are missing or inaccurate.	Model clearly relates to the real-world issue and helps the student visualize the natural phenomenon of flooding in a coastal community.	Model clearly relates to the real-world issue and helps the student visualize the natural phenomenon of flooding in a coastal community. Key elements are labeled correctly.	
Model Construction and Design	Poor Construction and Design. Lack of planning.	The model is missing elements and labels are messy or absent. Minimal effort was put into planning.	Design is carefully constructedand shows some planning. Model is neat. Required elements are included.	Design is well thought out and executed. Creative use of materials and neat construction. Attention to detail and extra care was taken to design the model. Labels are neat.	
Presentation Preparation and SEL Competence	Student is not prepared for presentation and shows little empathy for victims of flooding.	Student presents basic, scientific information but does not discuss human impact of flooding.	Student correctly presents scientific concepts, has clearly prepared for the presentation. Student does express empathy for communities represented I the model.	Student has gone above and beyond to prepare an engaging presentation. Student explains the science in an interesting way, and also spends time expressing empathy and compassion for families that may have suffered	

Figure 2.3 Model and Presentation Rubric: Storm Surge.

Humans and the Environment   21

> **A Note to Teachers:** Rubrics are important assessment tools during problem-based learning. Ensure that you spend time discussing the expectations outlined in the rubric prior to scoring the students' models and presentations.

Elaborate

Now that you know a little about the devastation that flooding can cause, let's talk about some positive, preventative actions that people can take to be prepared for natural disasters like these. What should people do if they know that a storm is heading toward their community and that flooding may be a result?

Be Prepared

As Winston Churchill once said, "Those who fail to plan, plan to fail." Planning ahead is always a good idea. In the case of weather-related emergencies, preparing before the fact may save lives. Here are some actions and decisions that you and your family can take beforehand in order to stay safe during a flood: (1) make a plan for how you will receive emergency notifications, (2) decide how you will communicate with your family members during and immediately after the emergency, and (3) decide where you will go if you need shelter during a storm. Making and communicating these decisions to all the members of your household is a critical step toward the development of your family's emergency plan. Another important part of emergency preparation is having an emergency kit available. This kit should have enough water to last you three days and some non-perishable food items. The emergency kit might also contain supplies such as a flashlight, a first-aid kit, and extra batteries.

> **SMALL GROUP DISCUSSION**
> What essential items will you include in your family's emergency kit? Justify your answers.

Safety First

According to ready.gov, there are actions that people can take to stay safe during a flood. One of the most important things to remember during a flood is the importance of staying away from flood waters. Evacuate the area immediately if authorities have determined that an evacuation is necessary. Seek a safe shelter. Never drive through flood waters. Check out: https://www.ready.gov/floods to know what people should do before, during, and after a flood.

Turn Around, Don't Drown

One of the preventative actions for staying safe during a flood is explained in a simple phrase: "Turn around; don't drown!" What does this mean to you? How would you explain this to a friend who wanted to play or swim in a "river" caused by flood waters?

Elaborate Activity

Write your own "catch phrase" that might help people stay safe during a flood. Create a marketing poster to advertise your safety slogan. Present your idea to your class and help your teacher create a flood safety bulletin board in the classroom (Figure 2.4).

Evaluate

Based on the information that you learned during this project, design a safety plan for responsible decision-making during a flood. Be creative in how you present your plan. Use powerful writing and informative text to communicate your plan effectively. You might consider: creating a pamphlet with informative text and visuals, writing a newsletter with information and instructions, or writing a script for an informative video presentation and filming the video. Share your plan with your teacher, classmates, and family members. Be bold and take the initiative to help others learn about how to stay safe during storms.

Writing Informational Texts

Focus on introducing the topic, and creating an organizational structure in which your related ideas are grouped together in a way that supports your purpose. Clearly state your purpose and reasons for writing. Support any reasons with examples and facts. Use precise language. Write a concluding statement (Figure 2.5).

When you are preparing your final writing product, make sure to keep your purpose and audience in mind. Ensure that you work with your teacher and peers to brainstorm ideas, plan, write, revise, edit, and rewrite. Do your best to present the final product in a format worthy to be published and shared. Writing is a process, and it is difficult, but it can be fun and worthwhile too. In this case, the words you write will help people. When writing gets tough, remember why you are doing it in the first place. Writing is hard, but you can do it. When you write about something, you are learning more about the subject, your audience, and yourself. According to William Zinsser, an expert on the topic, writing helps us think. Writing helps us learn by clarifying what we know about a subject (Zinsser, 1993) (Table 2.3).

> **A Note to Teachers:** If you or your students have lived through the trauma of a flooding event, you may consider focusing on the "engage" and "exploration" components of this project. Focus on encouraging healing through creative writing, and avoid triggering any post-traumatic stress responses.

Humans and the Environment 23

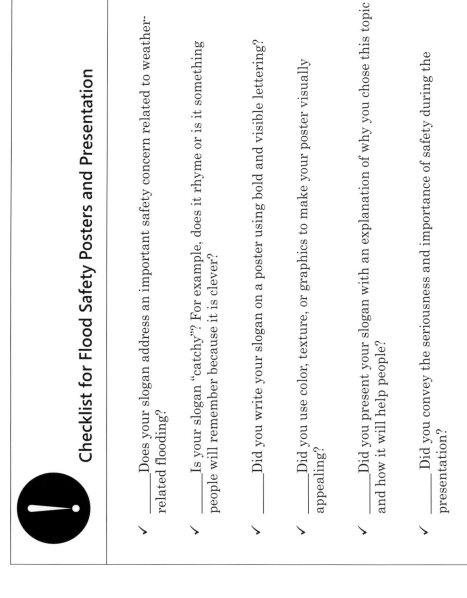

Figure 2.4 Self-Assessment – Checklist for Flood Safety Slogan Posters and Presentations.

Copyright material from Season Mussey (2022),
Social-Emotional Learning Through STEAM Projects, Grades 4–5, Routledge

Figure 2.5 The Writing Cycle.

Table 2.3 Rubric for Safety Plan: Informative Text

Below Expectations	**Approaching Expectations**	**Meets Expectations**	**Exceeds Expectations**
Student fails to create a written safety plan.	Student introduces the topic. Some of the ideas are grouped together and some examples are included. Student worked through some stages of a writing process. Student presents a final product that requires additional revisions before it can be published.	Student introduces topic clearly, groups ideas together, and supports points with evidence or examples. A concluding statement is present. The student addresses the topic of creating a flood safety plan. The student worked through a writing process to create a written, publishable final product.	Student introduces topic clearly, groups ideas according to purpose, and uses precise language. Student has considered audience when writing. Any ideas are supported with examples or facts. A concluding statement is present and reiterates purpose. Student voice shares a clear message about flood safety planning. There is evidence that the student worked through a writing process. The final product is in a publishable and creative format, such as a pamphlet, paper, or script.

Extension Activities

When diving into research on flooding in our communities, there is so much to learn. Beyond understanding the human response in stories and poems, facts about storm surge, and safety planning, there is scientific research to read, and humanitarian efforts to acknowledge. Keep reading for additional resources and extension activities related to this topic.

A Scientific Study: Flooding and Coral Reefs

The consequences of flooding, especially a flood as large as Hurricane Harvey, could be felt hundreds of miles from its epicenter. One of the effects of this particular flood was the pollution of a coral reef nearly 100 miles from the Texas coastline. In 2021, a group of scientists published a scientific paper about this phenomenon. This paper helps us understand some of the long-distance impacts of flooding on the environment, including ecosystems far from shore. Students can access and read the scientific paper for details on the study's purposes, methodology, and findings. The full citation for the paper is:

Shore, A., et al. (2021) On a Reef Far, Far Away: Anthropogenic Impacts Following Extreme Storms Affect Sponge Health and Bacterial Communities. *Frontiers in Marine Science.*
DOI: 10.3389/fmars.2021.608036

An Interview: Scientists in Action

In order to better understand some of the scientific information presented in the study, students can watch an interview with one of the study's leading scientists, Dr. Adrienne Correa. In this YouTube video, Dr. Correa discusses how the extreme flooding events on the Texas coast affected the Flower Garden Banks National Marine Sanctuary with bacteria from human fecal waste. In the video, Dr. Correa says that scientists were shocked by these findings. Watch the video entitled "Human flooding polluted reefs more than 100 miles offshore" here: https://www.youtube.com/watch?v=POPcfhy2Rrc

Think About It...

One thing that we learn from this study is that run-off from the Hurricane Harvey flood of 2017 and another flood in 2016 carried human waste to coral reefs, 100 miles offshore. This far-reaching, negative consequence of the flood is another example of how humans negatively affect their environment, even unintentionally.

Small Group Discussion Questions

Based on what you learned from the video, discuss the following:

1. What can we do to make a positive difference or reverse some of the effects of pollution on land and marine environments?
2. Why do you think the scientists were shocked to learn that the flood's impacts had reached all the way to the reefs? Discuss how the role of the "element of surprise"

in science. In particular, discuss how the findings from this study will influence the next study. (Rewatch the video for ideas.)

> If you could ask Dr. Correa any other questions about the study, what would you ask? Write three to five interview questions.

A Humanitarian Response: Heroes with Boats

There is no doubt that flooding can have lasting consequences for individuals, communities, and our environment. We have seen several negative examples of these consequences through the first-hand experiences and the written work of student poets and research scientists. There are also positive effects of flooding. One of the most memorable, positive outcomes from the Houston floods of 2016 and 2017 was the creation of the Louisiana Storm Patrol, a team of individuals who came together to rescue people during the storms. This group of humanitarian volunteers drove from Louisiana to Texas, pulling their boats on trailers. Once they arrived in Texas, they got in their boats and braved the flood waters to rescue many lives from flooded homes and businesses. They mobilized then and are an organized non-profit now. Today, The Louisiana Storm Patrol works hard to serve those in need during times of disaster. They believe that "we can all rise high together and be part of the solution bringing real change to families and communities" (www.lousiananstormpatrol.com).

Think About It...

How can you be a part of the solution and bring real change to your family and community? Think of three positive ways that you can serve those around you this week. Identify your own strengths and consider how you can use your abilities to help others. For example, are you good at math and can you help your little brother or sister with their math homework? Are you supportive of others and can you write a note thanking a teacher who helped you? Are you good at soccer and can you help your team improve by working hard at your next practice?

Extension Activities

If you have loved learning about the problem of weather-related disasters like flooding, and want more, consider completing one or more of the following additional activity ideas.

1. Create an interactive model or map (poster or digital) showing some of the immediate and long-lasting impacts of flooding. Find a way to show where and how much water there is before/during/after a flood. Consider using Houston or another flood-prone city as an example.
2. Publish a Flood Safety guide for your neighborhood in multiple languages. This guide should help individuals and communities make responsible decisions during a weather-related flooding disaster. Focus on safety and human preparation.
3. Using paint or other media, collectively create a mural or other artwork showing the emotions that you experienced when reading about and learning about the consequences of flooding.
4. Publish a classroom collection of original poetry about flooding.

Conclusion

Based on what you have learned about flooding, let's revisit the initial essential questions. Think about how your answers have changed based on what you have learned.

Essential Questions, Revisited

1. What are the immediate and long-lasting consequences of weather-related flooding on environments?
2. What are some positive and negative outcomes of flooding on land and offshore?
3. How can we help people before, during, and after weather-related floods?
4. What are some other ways that we could reduce the effects of flooding on human communities?

Final Reflection

Journal Prompt: What do you know now that you didn't know before? Based on what you read, how likely is it that you would know what to do during flooding caused by a storm? What are some of the positive effects of flooding on communities?

Project #2: Climate Change and Communication

Academic Learning Objectives

Project #2 will help students build on what they have learned about weather and climate in Grade 3. They will review some basic knowledge and skills. Building on that knowledge, students will begin to look at how human behavior can change the climate on earth as they focus on a study of earth and human activity. In particular, they will begin to understand how the uses of renewable and non-renewable energy sources affect the environment. Students will go deeper in their understanding of a systems approach to interactions in the natural environment as they investigate changes in the distribution of water on earth. Students will:

a) Differentiate between weather and climate.
b) Use multiple sources to research and define *ice age* and discuss how extreme climates and climate change can affect living organisms in ecosystems.
c) Differentiate between renewable and non-renewable energy sources. Explain how human choice has affected climate on earth.
d) Explain how and why the climate on earth is changing today. Create a visual representation, such as a graph or model, of the changes in the distribution of water on earth with a focus on glaciers and sea levels.

SEL Competencies

a) **Self-awareness:** Students will select an environmental topic that they are passionate about. As they gather relevant information about this issue, they will develop interests and gain a sense of purpose. They will answer questions about their role in finding solutions to important issues such as global warming.

b) **Responsible decision-making:** During this project, students will communicate their ideas effectively using written and oral language. With each opportunity to communicate, they will demonstrate open-mindedness as they identify solutions for social problems.

c) **Social awareness:** Students will recognize strengths in others when they identify the qualities of individuals who are taking climate action.

Essential Questions

1. What is the difference between weather and climate?
2. How does the climate on earth affect populations of organisms?
3. How is the climate changing on earth today? Why?
4. What are the consequences of global warming?
5. How can kids use communication to change the world and make a difference in global issues such as climate change?

Stages of Inquiry

Before you begin to move through the five stages of inquiry for Project #2, discuss your answers to the essential questions with your small group. What do you think you already collectively know about this issue? What evidence do you have to support what you think you know?

Introduction to the Problem

What is the weather like today where you live? Was the weather the same today as it was yesterday or did it change? Visit the website www.weather.com. In the search box at the top of the screen, type in your city name or zip code. Look at the ten-day forecast for your city. What is the average high temperature for your city for the next week? What is the average low temperature for your city for the next week? Work in your small group to find the answers. **Discuss:** Based on this information, how should we dress? What activities would be appropriate for the weather this week?

Weather versus Climate

Weather changes daily. Today it might be rainy and cold, but tomorrow, and for the next few weeks, it might be warm and sunny. When you study weather over time, you begin to observe patterns. Weather patterns in a particular geographic area over long periods of time determine the climate. The climate on earth can change due to atmospheric conditions. Take, for example, the various ice ages that have occurred over time. Scientists have determined that there have been at least five major ice ages in our earth's history. Ice ages were periods on earth when the weather was consistently cold. During an ice age, there is often snow and icy precipitation that accumulates on the ground in massive quantities. Sheets of ice and snow called glaciers can form and move slowly over land, covering large geographical areas. When we study geography and geology, we realize that the glaciers of the past have left us with clues about when and where ice ages occurred.

Ice Ages

Scientists, called geologists, study the earth's surface and the history of the earth's surface, by looking at rocks and land formations on the surface and buried in layers of the earth. These layers have stories to tell. One of the stories that they tell is the story of the ice ages. An ice age is a long period of time on earth when temperatures are colder, there is more icy and snowy precipitation, and more glaciers form on the earth's surface. Scientists can tell us when and where glaciers occurred and what animals and plants lived during these times. This is because massive ice formations and glaciers affect the earth's surfaces. We can also learn about the plants and animals that lived during the ice ages from paleontologists – scientists who study fossils buried in the earth's layers.

> **Creative Exercise:** Imagine the challenges of living in a glaciated world, on the ice. Where would you live? What would you wear? What would you need to survive? What might be some of the benefits and challenges? Now, write a diary entry *or* draw a picture from the perspective of a child who lives in this frozen world.

Canada Then and Now

Based on a study of geology, scientists have learned that 20,000 years ago Canada was covered with ice (Lorentz, 2008). What does Canada look like now? While there are still some very cold places in Canada, especially in the winter, it is no longer completely covered with ice. Today, although we are still in the Holocene Period of the Quaternary Ice Age, the earth's climate, overall, is warmer than it was 20,000 years ago (Lorentz, 2008). The ice that once covered Canada has melted. The climate has changed (Figure 2.6).

Climate Change

Climate change is not a new phenomenon. The earth's climate has always changed due to volcanic eruptions, changes in the earth's orbit, and receiving more or less energy from the sun. Ocean currents can also change the climate. These are natural sources of climate change. Humans can also affect the environment, including climate change. In the past 100 years, the average temperature on earth has risen. This warming trend is caused in part by natural phenomena and in part by human choices.

Humans use fuel as energy. We have chosen, for years, to use coal, oil, natural gas, and other fossil fuels as our primary sources of energy. We fuel our cars with gasoline. We heat our homes with natural gas or electricity and cool our homes with electric energy. Much of our electric energy comes from the burning of coal. We use fossil fuels in airplanes (jet fuel), to make our streets (asphalt), and even to make plastic and some clothing (petroleum products). Fossil fuels are non-renewable energy sources. Renewable energy sources exist.

30 Humans and the Environment

 What is an Ice Age? If you answered that it is a collection of animated movies about a wooley mammoth, saber-tooth tiger, and a sloth, then you would be correct…but that it not the ice age that we are talking about today.

In this assignment, you are going to research the term **ICE AGE**. As you gather relevant information about what an ice age is, you also will find some answers about how an ice age affects life on earth as well as the distribution of natural resource, including water.

 For the first part of this assignment, read the article and watch the video, *"Ice Age"* found here:

https://www.history.com/topics/pre-history/ice-age

Answer the following questions. You may have to collect additional information from other sources.

1. In the video, Professor S. James Gates from the University of Maryland says that "at times, the conditions here (on earth) have been inhospitable." Give an example of one of those times. What made life on earth difficult?
2. Define ice age. What are some characeistics of ice ages?
3. How many ice ages have there been on earth? How have ice ages changed earth?
4. Who studies ice ages? (type of scientist)
5. What are some ways that humans can survive ice ages? How can humans adapt to harsh climates?

 Key Words: *ice age, inhospitable, adpat, characteristics, climate*

EXTENSION ACTIVITY: RESEARCH PROJECT

THE HISTORY OF ICE AGES

Find multiple sources to answer the following questions about ice ages. How many have occurred on earth? What evidence do we have to prove that ice ages occurred? Are we in an ice age now? Present your findings in an informative paper about ice ages. Make sure to introduce the topic, organize your main ideas in paragraphs, provide examples and facts to support your main ideas, and write a concluding statement. List your references at the end of your paper.

Figure 2.6 Ice Age Assignment.

Renewable energy includes power from solar, water, and wind sources. Humans have a choice in what kind of energy we use. That choice has consequences.

> Visit the U.S. Energy Information and Administration's website to see the primary sources of energy consumption in the United States:
> https://www.eia.gov/energyexplained/renewable-sources/

Small Group Discussion Questions

1. What does it mean to be a non-renewable energy source? Give some examples.
2. What does it mean to be a renewable energy source? Give some examples.
3. What % of the energy in the USA comes from renewable sources? What is the primary renewable energy that we use?
4. How much of our energy comes from the burning of fossil fuels (petroleum/crude oil, coal, natural gas)?

Actions and Consequences

When humans make a choice, the environment often faces the consequences. Sometimes it takes decades or even centuries for humans to understand what those consequences might be. This was true of the case of humanity's choosing fossil fuels as our primary energy sources. It wasn't until the Industrial Revolution that we started seeing warming trends as a result of burning fossil fuels. So, what changed? What happened during the Industrial Revolution that allowed us to burn enough fuel that it would change the environment? In this project, we will explore some human choices and environmental outcomes related to climate change. We will research the facts and find answers to difficult questions. Once you know the answers, you have a choice. We will see how some kids are choosing to take climate action, raising their voices in defense of humanity, and making positive change for generations to come. Will you join in their cause?

Engage

The air temperature on earth is 2.12 degrees Fahrenheit warmer than it was in the year 1900 (NASA, 2021c) (https://climate.nasa.gov/evidence/). The temperatures on earth are getting warmer, on land and in the oceans, where much of this excess heat is absorbed. As a result of increasing temperatures, ice-sheet mass in the sea and the glacial coverings of land are shrinking. When this happens, the ocean levels rise. The sea has risen 8 inches (20cm) in the last century (Nerem et al., 2018).

There are organizations that record and monitor air temperatures, glacial coverings, snow cover, and sea level. The data is being collected. Scientists all over the world analyze and compare the data. They study the trends and changes over time. Based on analysis of data and results that are communicated globally, conclusions are made. The conclusions, based on this evidence, are that the earth's climate is changing. There is a consensus, based on factual evidence, that these things are true: global temperatures are increasing, glacial cover and sea ice is shrinking, sea levels are rising (Oreskes, 2004).

Engage Activities

Visit NASA's website on climate change. Go here: https://climate.nasa.gov/

In your small group, search this website and others to find the answers to the following questions:

1. What evidence do we have that climate change is happening?
2. Why is the climate changing?
3. What are the effects of climate change on earth?
4. Are there any solutions?
5. How does knowing this information make you feel?
6. What do you want to do about it?

Additional Resources for Students

- For more evidence, facts about climate change, and Vital Signs of the Planet, go here: https://climate.nasa.gov/evidence/
- For global climate change indicators from the National Centers for Environmental Information, go here: https://www.ncdc.noaa.gov/monitoring-references/faq/indicators.php#warming-climate
- For global climate change impacts in the United States, go here: https://nca2009.globalchange.gov/
- For information about the coastal sensitivity to sea-level rise, go here: https://www.globalchange.gov/sites/globalchange/files/sap4-1-final-report-all.pdf
- To learn more about the science behind how Earth's climate is changing, go here: https://thesciencebehindit.org/how-is-earths-climate-changing/

Explore – Polar Bears, Pandas, and Other Animals

Global warming affects many living organisms on earth. Plants and animals, including humans, are being affected in negative ways because of global warming. For example, the polar bear has become vulnerable to climate change as its habitat is shrinking due to melting ice sheets. Polar bears depend on sea ice for a place to hunt, rest, and roam; the sea ice is where polar bears find their preferred food: seals. Fortunately, polar bears have adapted to a loss of hunting ground and are able to consume other forms of prey, but they are still profoundly negatively affected when their home literally melts. Imagine if your home just melted into the sea. What would you do? The polar bears are not the only species of plants and animals being forced to adapt or become extinct due to climate shifts (Figure 2.7).

Another example of animals affected by climate change is the giant panda (WWF, 2021). Bamboo makes up 90% of a panda's diet. As bamboo plant growth is affected by increased air temperatures, so is a panda's ability to find food. This causes panda populations to migrate

Figure 2.7 *Save-the-Polar-Bears Banner.*

to areas with healthy bamboo forests, areas where humans may have already taken over habitats with agriculture and other economic pursuits. As you can see, there are many direct and indirect outcomes of global warming on plant and animal life.

Explore Activity

> **SAVE THE ANIMALS CAMPAIGNS**
>
> In your small group, explore the World Wildlife Federation's (WWF) website on wildlife and climate change. Go here: https://www.worldwildlife.org/initiatives/wildlife-and-climate-change
>
> Choose *one* animal to research. Create a "SAVE THE _____!" campaign poster and presentation. In your presentation, share ways in which climate change directly and indirectly affects the population of the organism that you chose. Discuss the geographic region where this animal lives. With visuals, such as maps and photographs, show your class what you have learned. Discuss the animals' vulnerability factors, and research ways that humans can reduce threats to these animals. Convince your class that we must work together to save the animals. Work together with a small team. Identify one another's strengths and divide and conquer the workload (Figure 2.8).

Rubric – Save the Animal Campaign

See Table 2.4.

Explain

One of the reasons that the problems caused by climate change are difficult to solve is because the solutions require global cooperation and participation. Humans must understand and believe that global warming is a problem worth solving. How can we convince people who doubt the critical need to take climate action now?

The Need for Scientific Literacy

Humans must have some basic scientific literacy around climate issues. One of the most common misconceptions that arises when humans discuss climate change solutions is the distinction between weather and climate. Some humans don't believe that there is climate change or global warming happening when they are living through a temporary snowstorm. They will ask: How can there be global warming when it is 30 degrees Fahrenheit outside? This question is problematic and shows a lack of understanding of the difference between the concepts of weather versus climate.

Explain Activity

Imagine that you meet someone who doubts the scientific evidence that demonstrates that global warming is happening. How would you change their mind? Create a plan to explain what you have learned about climate change. Start by differentiating between weather and climate. This

34 Humans and the Environment

Self-Assessment – Checklist for Save the Animal Campaign

https://www.worldwildlife.org/initiatives/wildlife-and-climate-change

> ___ Did you work in a small group?
> ___ Did you identify a group leader?
> ___ Did you define group member roles and individual tasks?
> ___ Did you ask your teacher for help when you needed it?
> ___ Did you use the WWF website on wildlife and climate change?
> ___ Did you choose ONE animal to research?
> ___ Did the group members with the greatest artistic abilities create a campaign poster?
> ___ Did you research how climate change affects the animal that you chose?
> ___ Did you discover the geographic region where this animal lives?
> ___ Did you find a map and/or pictures of the animal's habitat?
> ___ Did you research and record the animals' vulnerability factors?
> ___ Did you research ways that humans can reduce threats to these animals?
> ___ Did you work as a team to synthesize information and prepare the presentation?
> ___ Did you practice your presentation?
> ___ Did you present the required information and visuals during the presentation?
> ___ Did you convince your class to save the animals affected by global warming?

Figure 2.8 Self-Assessment – Checklist for Save the Animal Campaign.

Table 2.4 Rubric – Save the Animal Campaign

Below Expectations	**Approaching Expectations**	**Meets Expectations**	**Exceeds Expectations**
Students do not work well together. One student does most or all of the work. The presentation is missing essential elements.	Students choose one animal to study. They create a campaign poster and presentation. Some of elements are missing. Students list ways that humans can reduce risk, but lack acknowledgment of their personal role in this issue.	Students work together, dividing the workload equitably. They present a campaign to save the animal that they chose. The presentation includes a campaign poster, maps, photographs. Vulnerability factors are discussed with an example. Ways that humans can reduce threats are offered. Students demonstrate commitment to climate change action.	Students work together, identifying one another's strengths and dividing the workload equitably. They present an excellent campaign to save the animal that they chose. The presentation includes a campaign poster, maps, photographs, and a compelling argument of why the animal matters. Vulnerability factors are discussed with examples. Several solutions and ways that humans can reduce threats are offered. Students demonstrate commitment to climate change action. They recognize they play a role in reducing the negative impact of human choices on animal and plant life.

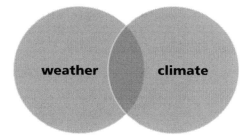

Figure 2.9 Venn Diagram – Weather versus Climate.

distinction is important as we attempt to communicate about global warming and other climate-related issues on earth. How would you explain the difference to someone? Write a paragraph to explain this topic. Use precise language to differentiate the two. Illustrate your paragraph with a Venn diagram to compare and contrast the two concepts: weather versus climate (Figure 2.9).

Using Visuals

If people understood the difference between climate and weather and were able to read basic graphs and charts showing some of the devastating effects of climate change, they may be more willing to work together toward change. In your small group draw two maps to model glacial melt. Draw two pictures: a before picture and an after picture. Use the photographs of the Muir Glacier in 1941 and in 2004 as inspiration. See the photographs on the NASA climate change website (2021). Go here:

https://climate.nasa.gov/climate_resources/4/graphic-dramatic-glacier-melt/

If more people understood the realities of climate change on earth, then perhaps more people would be willing to work together to find solutions and take action. After all, one of the reasons that humans, as a species, have been so successful in adapting to harsh environments is our ability to cooperate and solve environmental problems. Professor John Shea from Stony Brook University describes this combination of human cooperation and behavioral variability for problem-solving as the quintessential feature of our species (https://kids.nationalgeographic.com/science/article/climate-change, 2021).

Elaborate

Scientists have determined some of the causes of climate change. This is good news. If we know the causes, we can find the solutions. One of the main causes of global warming is the greenhouse effect. The sun warms the earth. The atmosphere absorbs and uses some of the energy from the sun. The remaining energy is reflected away from the earth's surface. Some of that heat gets trapped in the atmosphere, like in a greenhouse for plants. This is a natural process. There are some gases, called greenhouse gases, that trap more heat than others. Some of the greenhouse gases, such as CO_2 are made from man's use of fossil fuels, such as coal and oil. This upsets the natural process and increases the rate of warming on earth. When the warming increases to the rate that we see today, there are dire consequences, including the examples that we have been studying: increasing temperatures, melting sea ice, increased sea levels, loss of habitat for animals, harsher conditions for plant growth, etc. (NASA, 2021b) (https://climate.nasa.gov/causes/).

Solutions

We said that if we know the causes, we can find the solutions. The good news is that we have found some (Nunez, 2019)! Some of the easier solutions include using less power per person and using clean energy whenever possible. Clean energy is renewable energy. In order to reduce the amount of greenhouse gas emissions that we produce as individuals and as countries, we must work together (Shaw, 2021).

One Person Can Make a Difference

If each person on earth could limit their power use to only 2,000 watts per year, then humanity could limit the effects (of global warming). The average amount of power that individuals use varies from country to country. For instance, the average American consumes 12,000 watts of power each year (National Geographic, 2020).

Now that you know the problem and the solutions, what can you do? As a student, is there anything that you can really say or do that would influence change on a global scale? You may think not, but students can make a difference too. One such student, a girl from

Sweden named Greta Thunberg, gained notoriety in 2018 when she walked out of school and refused to return. She sat on the steps of a government building in Sweden in an effort to raise awareness about and inspire change for the climate of earth. She did this for her and for your future. She was "on strike" for the climate! Watch this TED Talk entitled, "The disarming case to act right now on climate change" from the climate change activist Greta Thunberg. Listen to what happened when she found out about climate change when she was eight years old. Go here:

https://www.ted.com/talks/greta_thunberg_the_disarming_case_to_act_right_now_on_climate_change

Think About It...

A few of the things that she says in the video really make us think. One of the things that she says is that even though we know that this global catastrophe is happening, "No one ever talked about it." Why do you think that people don't talk about it? She also says, "there are no gray areas when it comes to survival." What does this statement mean to you? Another thing that she says is, "The climate crisis has already been solved. We already have all the facts and solutions… All we have to do is to wake up and change… Instead of looking for hope, look for action."

Now, watch the video again. This time, instead of looking at what she says, notice *how* she says what she says. Greta is full of passion for this issue and compassion for humans, especially her generation and the generations that will follow. She has empathy for those who might be negatively impacted by global warming. Global issues tend to affect countries differently, based on financial wealth.. When the impacts of climate change affect crop growth in certain regions, populations of humans can experience famine. Greta cares deeply about the long-lasting effects of this crisis. She is angry that others don't feel the same way.

Class Discussion

What actions can your class and community take to reduce greenhouse gas emissions and take action for climate change? Do you understand Greta's feelings? How does thinking about this issue make you feel? Are there any issues that you are passionate about like Greta is passionate about this one?

> ### TAKE ACTION
>
> Review the website: a Blueprint for a Carbon Free-America. Go here: https://www.nationalgeographic.com/climate-change/carbon-free-power-grid/
> What are the alternative forms of energy that your state could/should be using?
> Write a letter to your state senator explaining the importance of using cleaner energy in your state.

Evaluate

Greta Thunberg isn't alone. There are millions of people around the world who are passionate about climate change, global warming, and inspiring action. Entire countries have recognized the global issue of climate change, and the potentially devastating consequences if we don't act now. In 2015, 196 of these countries signed the Paris Agreement (UNFCC), an international treaty on climate change. The treaty has specific aims to reduce the rate of global warming. Each country involved has agreed to make contributions toward global goals and communicate results with others. How important do you think it is for countries to work together on global issues, contribute to common goals, and communicate their outcomes with one another? Discuss your ideas with your class. You can read the Paris Agreement in multiple languages on the UN website here: https://unfccc.int/process-and-meetings/the-paris-agreement/the-paris-agreement

Final Thoughts

Climate change is an important global issue that requires immediate attention and action. We cannot solve this issue without global cooperation, communication, and commitment. Even though this problem is huge, one passionate person can make a difference. Could that person be you?

Final Reflection: Vlog

Make a 1–3-minute video reflecting on what you have learned during this project. State the importance of doing something now about climate change. Discuss ways that people are working together to make contributions toward global goals. Talk about how important it is to cooperate, communicate, and commit to change. Watch any of the following videos for inspiration:

- Greta Thunberg at the Climate Action Summit in 2019 at https://www.youtube.com/watch?v=u9KxE4Kv9A8
- Bill Nye speaking on climate change for National Geographic at https://www.youtube.com/watch?v=EtW2rrLHs08

Project #3: Food Insecurity
Academic Learning Objectives

In Project #3, students study food insecurity in America. They will use creative expression to summarize creative ways that communities are addressing this issue. With written reflection and response to journal prompts, students will process and communicate their feelings about hunger. Students will read and analyze interview transcripts. They will analyze interactive maps and use math problems with multiplication to draw conclusions. Students will:

a) Define the terms food insecurity, food waste, food deserts, and food distribution.
b) Draw a comic strip illustrating how people are helping redistribute food in more equitable ways.

c) Access interactive maps online. Students will locate maps for their region, analyze the information on the maps, and look for patterns. Using data from the maps, they will draw conclusions.
d) Use multiplication to solve simple math problems related to the real-world issue of cost of food per meal per family.
e) Read and analyze interview transcripts. They will discuss the feelings of the interviewee/participants using direct quotes as evidence.
f) Communicate effectively through reflective narrative writing to develop experiences using descriptive details.

SEL Competencies

a) **Social awareness:** Students will develop social awareness as they express concern and compassion for people who face food insecurity in America. They will also recognize unjust norms related to unequal food distribution and the locations of food deserts.
b) **Responsible decision-making:** Students will develop responsible decision-making as they recognize their role in community well-being and evaluate their potential to help address hunger in America.
c) **Self-awareness:** Students will develop self-awareness as they link feelings, values, and thoughts when they write about how they feel about this issue and what they will do as a result.
d) **Relationship skills:** Students will gain relationship skills as they observe the importance of seeking and asking for help when needed.

Essential Questions

1. What is food insecurity? Who is food insecure?
2. Is there enough food in our country to combat the hunger caused by food insecurity?
3. How much does it cost to feed a family?
4. What can I do to help my neighbors get the food they need so that they are happy and full?
5. What is the role of empathy in solving the issues of food insecurity in America?
6. What is the role of community and partnerships in solving food insecurity in America?
7. What are the social, emotional, and physical benefits of community gardens?

A Note to Teachers: Hunger and food insecurity is an issue that any American may face in their lifetime. You may have students who are experiencing hunger today. Please be sensitive to the physical and emotional needs of your students and their families. You may be the vital link to helping them find the resources that they need to thrive and fill their bellies.

Remember, "A hungry stomach cannot hear" (Jean de la Fontaine).

Stages of Inquiry
Introduction to the Problem

Did you know that Americans throw away thousands of pounds of perfectly edible food every single day? This food waste is common, especially in large metropolitan areas where there may be enough or even excess food (Feeding America, 2021a).

While food is being wasted, there are people in every county in America who do not have enough food to eat. When a person or a family doesn't know where their next meal will come from, it can be stressful and even scary. This condition, called food insecurity, is a reality for millions of Americans today. According to Feeding America (2021), the *coronavirus* pandemic starting in 2020, has exacerbated this problem. In 2021, there are more than 42 million Americans facing hunger. This includes 13 million children in America who do not know where their next meal is coming from. Many of these families rely on their local, community foodbank for the resources to fill their pantries and their bellies.

Part of the issue of food insecurity is not the amount of food available, but the unequal distribution of food and/or the availability of food. There are places in America where it is difficult to find a local food source. There is no grocery store near to the places where people live. We call these areas food deserts.

Fortunately, there are many people in America who care about making sure that people have enough to eat. These passionate, empathetic people care about others and work to solve the problem of food insecurity where they live.

In this project, you will learn about the issue of food insecurity and food distribution. You will meet two individuals who are working on the front lines to solve this issue. You will read about some organizations that work to minimize food waste and redistribute food to food deserts in their cities. There are solutions to the problem of food insecurity. In this project, you will start to understand how we can all help one another to make sure we have enough of what we need to be healthy and happy.

Engage

Have you ever wanted to be a superhero? Well, in the city of Austin, TX, there is a community of superheroes coming to the rescue of…*food*! The mission of this non-profit organization, Keep Austin Fed (2021), is to "reduce hunger and help the environment by connecting surplus food with our neighbors in need." The main way that they accomplish their mission is through the hard work of dedicated volunteers, such as Laura Cortez (Keep Austin Fed, 2021).

Laura Cortez volunteers with Keep Austin Fed because she is passionate about helping others. In her work, she has learned the value of food. You can read more about what Laura and other volunteers do to address food insecurity in Austin here: https://keepaustinfed.org/blog/laura-cortez

One of the most amazing things about Keep Austin Fed and other organizations like it is the massive impact that they can have on their communities. In 2000, this organization distributed, on average, 12,000 meals per week. The type of food that they redistribute includes healthy produce and prepared meals. The communities that they serve include low-income communities, those experiencing homelessness, seniors, women and children, veterans, people living with HIV/AIDS, at-risk teens, people with disabilities, people with mental illness, asylum seekers, and those in recovery (Keep Austin Fed, 2021).

So, what exactly do they do? How do they rescue the food? The work of food rescue happens because of partnerships between food suppliers and organizations who deliver food to those in need. Keep Austin Fed is the bridge, the distributors. The distributors are superheroes who drive to food sources, load their cars with rescued food, and then transport it from point A to point B before it spoils! For example, when a commercial restaurant or grocery store has a surplus of food, they call the Keep Austin Fed hotline. One of the volunteers comes to pick up the food and within the hour the food is delivered to another organization who will safely distribute it to people who would otherwise face food insecurity (Figure 2.10).

Explore

Now that we have met an organization that is working to end food insecurity, let's meet some individuals who work in this field. Read the following interviews. Then, in your class, discuss the following questions. Use direct quotes from the interviews to support your answers to some of the questions.

Class Discussion Questions

1. What motivates people to help others?
2. What did you learn about food insecurity and the people who face food insecurity from the interviews?
3. How can you make a difference and help those who might be food insecure in your own communities?
4. Both Paul and Sarah demonstrate concern, compassion, and empathy for populations who are facing food insecurity. What is empathy and how does it help us show concern and compassion for populations who are different from us?

Primary Source Document: Interview with Paul Garcia, 360 Outreach Center

(personal communication, June 6, 2021)

SEASON MUSSEY (SM): First of all, thank you so much for agreeing to this interview. I am so excited to learn from you about the important work that you are doing. So, please, tell my readers a little about who you are and what you do.

42 Humans and the Environment

Activity: Food Rescue Comic Strip

Read this...

It's late on Tuesday and the restaurant is almost closed. Most of the food has found a home in the bellies of the customers...But, something is terribly wrong!

OH NO!! In the back refrigerator is a surplus of 75 pounds of perfectly delicious, and untouched spaghetti. The cooks have made too much food today, and spaghetti is NOT on the menu tomorrow. The food is in danger of being thrown away and becoming food waste....but WAIT... There is a solution! HAVE NO FEAR...THE FOOD RESCUERS are here!

The food rescuers can take the food to the apartment community down the street. There is a food program available there. Every Wednesday night, this apartment community serves a hot and delicious FREE meal to all the residents and their friends, many of whom face food insecurity.

Thanks to the food rescuing volunteers, the food will not be wasted. It will feed people who may not have had access to a hot meal otherwise. By working together to redistribute food, the people in the restaurant, food rescue volunteers, and apartment managers have demonstrated how partnerships in communities can make a difference in the lives of friends and neighbors, and how together, we can solve the issue of food insecurity in America. These people are all superheroes in my book!

 Key Words: surplus, food waste, rescue, food insecurity, redistribute, partnerships

❖ **Activity:** Draw a comic strip illustrating the important steps, people and partnerships needed for the successful redistribution of food in communities. Who are the superheroes in your story? Label your comic strip and include captions and dialogue if needed.

Figure 2.10 Activity – Food Superhero Comic Strip.

PAUL GARCIA (PG): My name is Paul Garcia and I was born and raised in San Antonio, TX. My full-time job is an Education and Technology Specialist. My part-time job is a volunteer at 360 Outreach Center food distribution site.

SM: How did you get involved in this work and why do you do what you do? (In other words, what motivates you?)

PG: I got involved in this work through our church. We were visiting a church made up of a handful of adults and about 100 children. These children were from various, low-income housing complexes on the west and east side of San Antonio (Texas). I initially began volunteering to cook breakfast on Sundays and dinners on Wednesdays. These children did not eat on a regular basis during the summer since they were not attending school. Then a request for volunteers presented itself to assist with food distribution. I signed my family up and we have been volunteering for four years twice a month. My biggest motivation is the children. When I was a child there were times when my family went without food. I know how it feels to be hungry and I know how it feels to not know where your next meal is coming from. So, if I can fill someone's belly and pantry, I am going to do it and raise my children to also.

SM: Can you tell us a little about the communities where you serve?

PG: The community that we service is considered a low socioeconomic area of Bexar County. The clients we have are amazing people. They are made up of all backgrounds, education levels, and family size, but they all have a story. We serve about 40 families and 20 individuals.

SM: What are some challenges that you face in your day-to-day work?

PG: Some of the day-to-day challenges we face at the distribution site are:

a. The food bank does not have food for us to pick up.
b. The price of the food is constantly going up. We purchase the food we distribute at a discounted rate and as prices go up the amount of food we distribute decreases.
c. Some of our clients do not have refrigerators or stoves so we have to be aware of some of the (food storage and preparation) needs they might have.
d. Some of our clients do not have vehicles so we (must) deliver food.
e. It's hard to find volunteers.
f. We do not have enough refrigerators so it limits the amount of cold stuff we can give out.
g. The food bank is the only option we currently have to provide food for our distribution. If they turn us away then we cannot have a distribution.
h. There are times when the food we pick up from the food bank is spoiled and we have to throw it out.
i. COVID-19 created a small speedbump but we overcame it with touchless drive-through and walk-through distribution events.

SM: What is important for kids to know about food insecurity, distribution, and maybe even hunger or poverty?

PG: Kids need to know that food insecurity can happen to anyone. And if we have the ability to bless someone with their needs we should do it with a cheerful heart. Food distribution is hard work but it is necessary work that needs a constant supply of volunteers and donations.

SM: In your opinion, what can the average person do to get involved and help their communities?

PG: The average person is the person that can make the biggest change in the community. Getting involved and recruiting friends/family and creating a culture of volunteerism can move mountains when it comes to food insecurities.

SM: The United Nations has a goal of ending world hunger by the year 2030. How likely do you think this goal is to be achieved? In your opinion, what is it going to take to achieve this *huge* goal?

PG: The goal of ending world hunger by 2030 can be achieved but it is going to take all of us together to achieve it.

SM: What else would you like for me or my readers to know about this topic?

PG: One more thing that I would like everyone to know is that no one chooses to be hungry and whatever circumstance got them to this point is not important. What is important is ensuring that no one is hungry and we are following safe practices. We can make a difference in someone's life and it starts with one bag of food and a little bit of our time.

SM: Thank you for the amazing work you are doing in your community.

Primary Source Document: Interview with Sarah Combs, Sunrise Community Church Homeless Navigation Center

(personal communication, June 8, 2021)

SEASON MUSSEY (SM): First of all, thank you so much for agreeing to this interview. I am so excited to learn from you about the important work that you are doing. So, please, tell my readers a little about who you are and what you do.

SARAH COMBS (SC): My name is Sarah Combs and I am the Volunteer Coordinator and Donation Coordinator at Sunrise Homeless Navigation Center that operates out of Sunrise Community Church. I have been married to my awesome husband for 20 years and we have five kids together, so that keeps us pretty busy.

SM: How did you get involved in this work and what motivates you to do it?

SC: About four years ago I volunteered at an event to serve the homeless and left with the question, "How do you serve and help the chronically homeless?" Before that I didn't really have a lot of compassion for the people on the streets, but I wanted to learn how to love like God loves. Through that journey I ended up finding out about Sunrise. A few years later I started volunteering here. I love what Sunrise does and how we do it. We show up to help people get connected with the services they need to get out of their situation. That's our main focus. I am motivated to do this work because I feel like I'm living out God's love and heart for these people.

SM: Can you say more about the people that you serve?

SC: We serve people who live on the streets. We help connect them with services like food, clothing, hygiene supplies, mental health care, health care, food stamps, housing, and many other services. We serve any and everyone who comes asking. This is mostly people on the streets, but can also include people who are on the brink of homelessness.

SM: What are some of your biggest challenges?

SC: One of the biggest challenges we face is working on trying to get food to hand out. All of our food we serve comes from donations and that's not always consistent. We serve about 175 people per day Monday through Friday, so we need a lot of food each day.

SM: What is important for kids to know about food insecurity/distribution, homelessness, and/or hunger/poverty?

SC: Hunger is an issue, even in America. It's not limited to the third world and impoverished countries. You may not see it, but it's there; you just have to find it. I believe it will always be an issue but we can work towards reducing it.

SM: How can kids make a difference in their communities?

SC: I think the easiest thing is to reach out to an organization that already exists in the area that you are wanting to make a difference in. Get plugged in and learn from the people who are doing it.

SM: Is there anything else that you would like to say that I didn't ask you about during the interview?

SC: Each individual person you see living on the streets has their own story. They got in that situation in their own unique way and they have different issues that need to be addressed… If you can see these people as human beings like you that have had a rough life, it helps facilitate compassion and empathy which in turn leads us to treat them differently.

SM: Thank you for the amazing work that you are doing in our community.

Explain

Food insecurity and hunger is a real issue in America. Every year since 2011, the organization Feeding America has conducted a study to understand food insecurities in different parts of our country. Let's take a look and analyze some of the graphics in order to understand food insecurity across the USA.

Map Activity

1. Every year, Feeding America does a study to understand how many children are food insecure in America. They publish their data on an interactive map. Go to the interactive map called: Map the Meal Gap
   https://public.tableau.com/app/profile/feeding.america.research/viz/MaptheMealGap-ChildFoodInsecurity/ChildFoodInsecurity
2. Find your state on the map. Click on your state or use the drop-down menu to locate your state on the map. Look at the statistics for your state. Analyze the pie graph.
3. What % of your state is in food insecurity? _____
4. What % of children in your state are food insecure? _____
5. Next, find out what county you live in. Type in the name of your county.
    a) What is the food insecurity rate for your county? _____
    b) What is the cost per meal in your county? _____

46   Humans and the Environment

6. In your county, how much would it cost to feed a family of four for one week (three meals per day)? Do the math: How much would it cost? _____ Compare the cost to feed a family for one week in your county with another county in your state and with a county in another state.
7. Spend some time looking at different parts of the country. Notice where food insecurity is the highest. Notice where food insecurity percentages are lower.
8. **Class discussion:** Explain your observations to your class. In your explanation, try to use the terms food insecurity and food desert. Discuss why you think there are differences in food insecurity in different parts of the country?

Elaborate

Now that we have explored the issue of food insecurity in America, let's talk about one way to solve it. One way that seems to be making a difference, especially in urban communities is community gardens. According to Urban Harvest (2017),

> community gardens have become an important tool in the arsenal to combat food insecurity. Community gardening is simply the growing of healthy food on a piece of land in a specific community by those in the community to share among themselves and with others through donation. This plot of land can be privately owned, a church, school, hospital, community center and more recently, a vacant lot made available through the city.

The main benefit of a community garden is increasing the availability of healthy food in an area that may have previously been a food desert. But, there are social benefits as well.

When a community comes together to create a garden project, people learn to work together. They become socially aware of the needs of their community and begin to see their role in helping others. Growing food is empowering and builds efficacy around the idea of providing for oneself and others. Gardens can be a source of pride and a space for gathering and meeting together with others in the community. They are also beautiful green spaces and may provide a stark contrast to the concrete sidewalks and buildings in an urban center.

Similar to community gardens, school gardens can provide many benefits for those involved in planning, planting, and harvesting. Children can begin to appreciate the natural world with the hands-on experience that a school garden provides. As they work to plan, plant, and harvest the food from the garden, they learn about hard work, cooperation, and overcoming adversity. Gardens are also opportunities for family–school partnerships.

Design a Garden

As a culminating project, work with your class to design a community garden for your school or neighborhood. If you can, gather the resources and volunteers and build your garden. Consider researching the best and healthiest plants for your climate. Plant the plants. Learn how to water and harvest the food and distribute it in your community to those in need.

Humans and the Environment 47

NARRATIVE WRITING ASSIGNMENT: ASKING FOR HELP

Write a story about a time in your life when you needed help.

Write about what you needed. Did you ask for help? Why or why not? Was it difficult? What happened? What did you learn? How will you help others who are experiencing the same problem.

Use descriptive language and examples to tell your story.

Be specific and tell us who, what, when, where, and why.

Figure 2.11 Narrative Writing Assignment – Asking for Help.

Copyright material from Season Mussey (2022),
Social-Emotional Learning Through STEAM Projects, Grades 4–5, Routledge

48   Humans and the Environment

> **A Note to Teachers:** Many schools have a community garden already. If this is the case on your campus, use the project time to allow students to work in and improve the garden space that already exists. Consider getting parents involved and having a garden work-day. If this is a new project for your school community, keep in mind that this will be an ongoing, multi-year experience and that you can capitalize on multiple learning opportunities in and around this garden space. There are many resources for teachers for building gardens. Here are two excellent options:
>
> 1. A website: Resources for Building a School Garden from the Nature Conservancy (2021). Go here: https://www.nature.org/en-us/about-us/who-we-are/how-we-work/youth-engagement/nature-lab/school-garden-resources/
> 2. School Garden Resources from the Whole Kids Foundation (2021). Go here: https://www.wholekidsfoundation.org/school-gardens

Evaluate

In the blog article, "How to help your neighbors get by this summer and beyond," Paul Morello (2021) shares four easy ways to help our friends who might be facing food insecurity. He says that we can: (1) spread the word about food programs, (2) remind people that it is ok to need help, (3) volunteer at a local food bank, and (4) donate to food banks.

> **SMALL GROUP DISCUSSION**
>
> Why do you think that it is important to help others get access to the food that they need? What food resources are available in your community? Is there a food bank in your city? Is there a food program at your school? Why do you think that it is important to remind people that it is ok to need help? Have you ever needed help? What did you do? (See Figure 2.11 and Table 2.5.)

Table 2.5 Rubric for Narrative Writing Assignment

Below Expectations	Approaching Expectations	Meets Expectations	Exceeds Expectations
The author answers the questions in the prompt, but does not connect the ideas in a narrative story. Details are lacking and connections to big ideas are omitted.	Author writes about a time when they needed help. The author addresses some of the writing prompt but omits important details or lacks connection to the big ideas of helping others.	Narrative story is about a time when the author needed help. The author shares a memory using descriptive language and some details. The author talks about what they learned about helping others. There is a beginning, middle, and end.	Narrative story is about a time when the author needed help. Significant details and memories are shared. The author uses examples or dialogue. Descriptive language illustrates the event clearly. The author connects the event to what they have learned about helping others. There is a beginning, middle, and end to the story. The story is organized in paragraphs.

Final Thoughts

Food insecurity is a problem that we can solve. Continue to learn ways that you can help your friends and neighbors. Together, we can make a difference and fight hunger in America!

Note

1 NGSS is a registered trademark of WestEd. Neither WestEd nor the lead states and partners that developed the Next Generation Science Standards were involved in the production of this product, and do not endorse it.

Bibliography

Blake, E.S., & Zelinsky, E.A. (2018, May 9). National Hurricane Center Tropical Cyclone Report – Hurricane Harvey. [report] Retrieved on August 1, 2021 from https://www.nhc.noaa.gov/data/tcr/AL092017_Harvey.pdf.

Feeding America. (2021a). Hunger in America. [website]. Retrieved on August 2, 2021 from https://www.feedingamerica.org/hunger-in-america

Feeding America. (2021b). Map the Meal Gap. [Interactive Maps]. Retrieved on August 1, 2021 from https://public.tableau.com/app/profile/feeding.america.research/viz/MaptheMealGap-ChildFoodInsecurity/ChildFoodInsecurity

History.com Editors. (2015a). Ice Age [Article and Video]. A&E Television Network. Retrieved on July 31, 2021 from https://www.history.com/topics/pre-history/ice-age

History.com Editors. (2015b). Ice Age [quote] "An ice age is a period of colder global temperatures that features recurring glacial expansion across the Earth's surface." A&E Television Network. Retrieved on July 31, 2021 from https://www.history.com/topics/pre-history/ice-age

Jay, 4th Grade. (2017). Thief. Retrieved on October 25, 2021 from https://houstonfloodmuseum.org/jay-4th-grade/

Keep Austin Fed. (2021). Our Mission. [website] Retrieved on August 1, 2021 from https://www.keepaustinfed.org/who-we-are

Lorentz, K. (2008). Canada's Shrinking Ice Caps. NASA Langley Center. Retrieved on August 1, 2021 from https://www.nasa.gov/centers/langley/science/Canada_Ice.html

Louisiana Storm Patrol. (2020). Our Mission. Retrieved on May 6, 2021 from www.louisianastormpatrol.com.

Morello, P. (2021, July 6). How to Help Your Neighbor Get by This Summer and Beyond. [blog] Retrieved on August 1, 2021 from https://www.feedingamerica.org/hunger-blog/how-help-your-neighbors-get-summer-and-beyond.

NASA. (2021a). NASA: Climate Change and Global Warming. [website]. Retrieved on August 1, 2021 from https://climate.nasa.gov/

NASA. (2021b). The Causes of Climate Change. Causes. Vital Signs of the Planet [webpage]. Retrieved on August 1, 2021 from https://climate.nasa.gov/causes.

NASA. (2021c). Global Climate Change/Evidence. Retrieved on August 1, 2021 from https://climate.nasa.gov/evidence.

National Snow and Ice Data Center (NSIDS). (2021). What is the Current State of Glaciers Around the World? National Snow and Ice Data Center Website. Retrieved on August 2, 2021 from https://nsidc.org/

Nerem, R.S., Beckley, B.D., Fasullo, J.T., Hamlington, B. D., Masters, D., & Mitchum, G.T. (2018). Climate-change–driven Accelerated Sea-level Rise Detected in the Altimeter Era. *PNAS*, 2018. https://doi.org/10.1073/pnas.1717312115

Naomi Oreskes. (2004). The Scientific Consensus on Climate Change. *Science*. 3 December 2004, 306(5702), 1686. https://doi.org/10.1126/science.1103618

National Academic of the Sciences. (2021). How is Earth's Climate Changing? Retrieved on July 1, 2021 from https://thesciencebehindit.org/how-is-earths-climate-changing/

National Geographic. (2020). A Blue Print for a Carbon Free America. [Interactive Map] Retrieved on August 1, 2021 from https://www.nationalgeographic.com/climate-change/carbon-free-power-grid/

National Governors Association Center for Best Practices, Council of Chief State School Officers. (2010). *Common Core State Standards (Insert Specific Content Area If You Are Using Only One)*. Washington D.C.: Author. Retrieved on August 1, 2021 from http://corestandards.org/

National Snow and Ice Data Center Distributed Active Archive Center. https://doi.org/10.5067/MEASURES/CRYOSPHERE/nsidc-0530.001

Nature Conservancy. (2021). Resources for Building a School Garden. [website] *Nature.org*. Retrieved on October 25, 2021 from https://www.nature.org/en-us/about-us/who-we-are/how-we-work/youth-engagement/nature-lab/school-garden-resources/

NGSS Lead States. (2013). Next Generation Science Standards: For States, by States. Retrieved on August 1, 2021 from http://www.nextgenscience.org

NOAA. (2021). "How do we know the earth's climate is warming?" Global Climate Change Indicators. National Centers for Environmental Information (NCEI) [website]. Retrieved on August 1, 2021 from https://www.ncdc.noaa.gov/monitoring-references/faq/indicators.php#warming-climate

Nunez, C. (2019). Global Warming Solutions Explained [article]. Retrieved on July 1, 2021 from https://www.nationalgeographic.com/environment/article/global-warming-solutions.

Nye, B. (2015, Dec. 2). Climate Change 101. National Geographic. YouTube. [video]. Retrieved on June 28, 2021 from https://www.youtube.com/watch?v=EtW2rrLHs08

Ready.gov. (2021). Floods. [website]. Retrieved on August 1, 2021 from https://www.ready.gov/floods

Rice University. (2021, April 6). Human Flooding Polluted Reefs More Than 100 Miles Offshore. YouTube [video]. Retrieved on August 1, 2021 from https://www.youtube.com/watch?v=POPcfhy2Rrc

Robinson, D.A., Hall, D.K., & Mote, T.L. (2014). *MEaSUREs Northern Hemisphere Terrestrial Snow Cover Extent Daily 25km EASE-Grid 2.0, Version 1*. Boulder, Colorado USA.

Shaw, A. (2021). Climate Change. National Geographic. [article]. Retrieved on October 25, 2021 from https://kids.nationalgeographic.com/science/article/climate-change

Shore, A., et al. (2021). On a Reef Far, Far Away: Anthropogenic Impacts Following Extreme Storms Affect Sponge Health and Bacterial Communities. *Frontiers in Marine Science*, April 6, 2021, 1–16. https://doi.org/10.3389/fmars.2021.608036

The Houston Flood Museum. (2017a). Hurricane Harvey Exhibit. [museum archives]. Retrieved on August 1, 2021 from https://houstonfloodmuseum.org/category/hurricane-harvey/

The Houston Flood Museum. (2017b). The Ocean Is Wearing My Clothes: Student Stories and Poems [Archives - Houston Flood Museum]. Retrieved on August 1, 2021 from https://houstonfloodmuseum.org/category/hurricane-harvey/the-ocean-is-wearing-my-clothes-student-stories-and-poems/

The Weather Channel. (2021). weather.com [website]. Retrieved on July 1, 2021 from https://weather.com/

Thunberg, G. (2018, November). The Disarming Case to Act Right Now on Climate Change. *TedTalk*. Retrieved on June 14, 2021 from https://www.ted.com/talks/greta_thunberg_the_disarming_case_to_act_right_now_on_climate_change

Thunberg, G. (2019, September 3). We'll Be Watching You. Climate Action Summit. Retrieved on June 15, 2021. YouTube [video] from https://www.youtube.com/watch?v=u9KxE4Kv9A8

UNFCC. (2015). Paris Agreement. Retrieved on August 1, 2021 from https://unfccc.int/process-and-meetings/the-paris-agreement/the-paris-agreement

Urban Harvest. (2017). *Community Food Security by Community Gardening*. University of Houston. Office of Sustainability. [article] Community Food Security by Community Gardening - University of Houston. Retrieved on May 13, 2020 from https://www.uh.edu/sustainability/news/articles/2017/January/01202017UrbanHarvest.php

U.S. Climate Change Science Program. (2009). Coastal Sensitivity to Sea Level Rise. [report]. Retrieved on July 1, 2021 from https://www.globalchange.gov/sites/globalchange/files/sap4-1-final-report-all.pdf.

U.S. Global Change Research Program. (2009). Global Climate Change Impacts in the United States [report]. Retrieved on Juy 1, 2021 from https://nca2009.globalchange.gov/

Whole Kids Foundation. (2021). School Gardens [website]. Retrieved on October 25, 2021 from https://www.wholekidsfoundation.org/school-gardens

World Wildlife Federation. (2021). World Wildlife Federation Initiatives [website]. Retrieved on August 2, 2021 from https://www.worldwildlife.org/initiatives/wildlife-and-climate-change.

Writers in the Schools. (2021). Writers in the Schools [website]. Retrieved on August 1, 2021 from https://witshouston.org/

Zinsser, W. (1993). *Writing to Learn: How to Write and Think Clearly About Any Subject at All*. New York: Harper Perennial.

Chapter 3

Humans and Health

Introduction

When we think of human health, it is critical to think about holistic health: physical, mental, psychological, social, emotional, etc. Health is more than the absence of sickness. In the preamble to the Constitution of the World Health Organization (1946), healthy is defined as "a state of complete physical, mental, and social well-being and not merely the absence of disease of infirmity." The WHO speaks of health as wholeness, and a standard of health as a basic human right. When we see inequity in health standards across diverse religious, political, socioeconomic, ethnic, or racial communities, we all suffer. The WHO speaks about the relationship of health and peace and the danger of promoting health in one region while neglecting a people group across a real or imaginary border. Health is not limited to individual persons. We can also consider the health of the community. When we work both at individual and community levels to promote health, we see the greatest benefits for all. A focus on community health can prevent disease, and improve well-being, educational outcomes, economic stability, safety, and happiness. The health of individuals and communities reflects the health of our society. Humans must work together to achieve health for all.

Humans, as a species, have thrived, adapting to many environmental and societal challenges over time. We have already seen how humans have survived and thrived after storms and floods, in ice ages, and how we have helped community members live through hunger and food scarcity. Humans have shown remarkable resilience in the face of adversity.

Overview of Projects #4, #5, and #6

Chapter 3 endeavors to celebrate the resilient human spirit and commitment to physical, mental, and social-emotional health, against all odds. In Project #4, students look at case studies of resilience and motivation in the context of quarantines. If you lived through the global *coronavirus* pandemic of 2020–2021, you may have personal insight into this experience. In Project #4, students will first study the history of quarantines in America. Then, they will turn their attention to the present day, and learn about some of the heroes of

DOI: 10.4324/9781003247449-3

the 2020 quarantine. In the most recent quarantine, as well as in our past, students will learn how humans found creative ways to connect and serve their friends and neighbors, even in isolation. Students will discuss ways that people have managed to stay mentally, socially, and emotionally healthy when isolation is the only way to protect their physical health. The human quality of resilience is defined and explored.

In Project #5, students will study how humans have worked toward living peacefully, creatively finding common ground, and occasionally solidifying their commitments to peace using written communication in the form of treaties and other important documents. Students will define what peace means to them and consider the role peace plays in their social and emotional health.

Finally, in Project #6 students will study healing. The human body has a remarkable mechanism for healing in our immune system. Human communities, similarly, have strived to find ways to heal, using conventional systems, but also in unconventional ways, such as using art. In Project #6, students answer the questions: What can hurt a community? How can humans use art to heal? How is physical healing similar to or different from community healing (Table 3.1)?

Project #4: In Quarantine: Case Studies of Resilience and Motivation

Academic Learning Objectives

Students will:

a) Identify reasons for quarantines in history and the positive and negative effects of isolation on human physical, social, emotional, and mental health.
b) Define health and describe what humans need to thrive.
c) Read about the history of quarantine. Explain the events in a historical context giving examples from the text.

SEL Competencies

a) **Self-awareness:** As students look at stories of individuals who share their strengths with others, students will reflect on their own ability to do the same. In doing so, they will begin to recognize their strengths and limitations.
b) **Social awareness:** Students will recognize the situational demands and opportunities that exist during quarantine. They will observe how individuals used these situational demands to serve others, even strangers, who they expressed concern for. Students will discuss times where their unique situations offered them the opportunity to help others. Students will reflect on their role to promote personal, family, and community well-being in certain situations.
c) **Responsible decision-making:** Students will discuss how humans worked cooperatively to find solutions to problems that existed during quarantines.

Table 3.1 Overview of Projects #4, #5, and #6, and Their Academic Standards and SEL

Project	Target Academic Standards For 4th and 5th Grades	Targeted SEL Core Competencies
4 – In Quarantine: Case Studies of Resilience and Motivation	National Health Education Standards (2019) NHS 2.5.6 technology and the effects on health NHS 1.5.2 Identify examples of emotional and social health NHS 1.8.3 Analyze how the environment influences health Common Core Standards CCSS.ELA-LITERACY.RI.4.3 CCSS.ELA-Literacy W.4.2, W.5.2	**Self-awareness:** Recognize strengths and limitations **Social awareness:** Recognize situational demands and opportunities and reflect on one's role to promote personal, family, and community well-being **Responsible decision-making:** Work cooperatively to find solutions; evaluate the impact of decisions on communities **Relationship skills:** Effective communication; seek or offer support and help when needed
5 – Peace and Human Health	National Health Education Standards NHS 1.5.2, 1.5.3 Common Core Standards R1.4.1, R1.5.9 W.4.4, W.5.4 SL.4.1, 4.2, SL 5.1, 5.2, 5.4, 5.9 National Core Art Standards Cr – Creating, Anchor #1	**Self-awareness:** Identify emotions; recognize how emotions influence their behavior **Self-management:** Set collective goals with personal agency towards meeting these goals **Social awareness:** Understand the perspectives of other people; recognize when historical or current situations require peace-keeping individuals or collective strategies **Relationship skills:** Observe how online communities are using relationships to promote cross-cultural communication, understandings, and peace **Responsible decision-making:** Reflect on the individual's role in communities, classrooms, and homes
6 – Healing and Art	National Core Art Standards Cr – Creating, Anchor #2 Cn – Connecting, Anchor #10 Re – Responding, Anchor #8 Common Core Standards CCSS.ELA-LITERACY.W.4.3, W.5.3 CCSS.ELA-LITERACY.SL.4.1, SL.5.15.1 NHS 1.5.2	**Responsible decision-making:** Demonstrate curiosity and open-mindedness. Use critical thinking in school and recognize how it is used outside of school **Relationship skills:** Communicate effectively, show leadership, resolve conflicts, problem-solve collaboratively

They will evaluate the impact of these decisions on the health of individuals and communities.

d) **Relationship skills:** Students will look at the effects of technology on communication, especially during times of isolation in quarantine. They will identify examples of people seeking and offering help when needed.

Essential Questions

1. Define health. What do humans need to survive? Why do you think feeling a sense of love and belonging is so important?
2. What is a quarantine? What are some of the positive and negative consequences of quarantines on human health (individual and community)?
3. How have humans used technology creatively to connect to one another during quarantine and other times of isolation? How does using communication technologies support our social-emotional well-being?
4. What is resilience and why is it important?
5. What are some factors that help humans overcome difficult obstacles?
6. How can one person's decisions affect the health of an entire community?

Stages of Inquiry
Introduction to the Problem

The word quarantine, which literally means 40 days (Merriam-Webster, 2021), has come to mean much more to those of us who lived through the *coronavirus* pandemic of 2020. Many people in America and around the world experienced a quarantine, an enforced time of staying home to stop the spread of an infectious disease. In some places, people stayed home by choice. In other situations, people experienced an enforced time of isolation. In both cases, however, the purpose of this quarantine was to prevent the spread of the infectious disease called COVID-19.

Even though we know that the purpose of a quarantine is for the greater good of public health, it is never easy to stay isolated from friends and family. Humans depend on one another for companionship, help, friendship, love, and to meet our deep need for feeling like we belong (Maslow, 1943). So, while the quarantine may have protected our physical health, it may have been challenging for our social-emotional and mental well-being. There is more to health than our physical bodies (Figure 3.1).

A Note to Teachers: Please be careful with how you introduce the topic of quarantine. Many students who experienced quarantine in 2020 may associate the term with trauma and isolation. You may select to study only the historical aspects of quarantine and focus on the positive outcomes and helpers, rather than relive the crisis. As Mr. Rogers' mother told him, "In times of crisis, look for the helpers."

Activity: A Picture of Health

The World Health Organization (1946) defines healthy as:

"a state of complete physical, mental, and social well-being and not merely the absence of disease of infirmity."

Think about it…

Do you agree with this definition of healthy? Define the word HEALTH:

_____

_____

_____

Key Terms:

health, infirmity, physical, mental, social, emotional, community

❖ Draw a picture of a person, family, or community that is healthy. Consider the importance of physical, mental, social, emotional, and community health before you draw. Be prepared to share your picture of health with your small group.

Figure 3.1 A Picture of Health.

Quarantines in America: A Part of Our History

Quarantine, and the social isolation that results, is very difficult for humans; yet, 2020 is not the first time that Americans have experienced these challenges. In this project, you will read a brief history of quarantine in America. You will learn about how quarantine prevented the spread of plague in coastal cities in the 14th century. You will review the first legislative acts sanctioning quarantine in America. You will learn how people have used their creativity and the technology available to overcome the trials of this difficult experience.

Whenever humans face adversity, such as the adversity that they face during any quarantine, stories of resilience, motivation, and compassion will emerge. Let's learn about how humans creatively used technology to remain connected to one another during the global pandemic of 2020–2021. Let's learn from those who overcame great obstacles to continue to help themselves and others meet that deep need to belong, even while social distancing from friends and family.

Engage

Did you know that 2020 is not the first time that Americans have experienced quarantine?
   Read about the history of quarantine in America here: https://www.cdc.gov/quarantine/historyquarantine.html

Engage Activity

Create a timeline of important events during the history of quarantine. Include some of the significant epidemics or pandemics that have warranted the need for quarantine and public health legislations. Include: 14th-century quarantines, early American quarantine events, late 19th- century events, the public health service act, and other important dates and events. Create a parallel timeline to show some of the most significant communications technologies and when they existed. Make sure to include the big four communication technologies: telephone, radio, television, and Internet. You can also include less obvious technology such as simple pencil and paper for letter writing, and the establishment of the postal service or telegrams (Figure 3.2).

Class Discussion

Discuss with your class how the available technologies during different time periods may have helped people thrive during the social isolation caused by quarantines. Use specific examples from your reading and research and refer to your timeline for a visual. For example, what technology was available during the cholera outbreaks in the late 19th century? How do you think communication helped people stay healthy? Compare technology then to the many communication technologies that were available in 2020. How does modern technology affect how we stayed connected and healthy during 2020? What are some positive and negative aspects of modern communication technologies?

58 Humans and Health

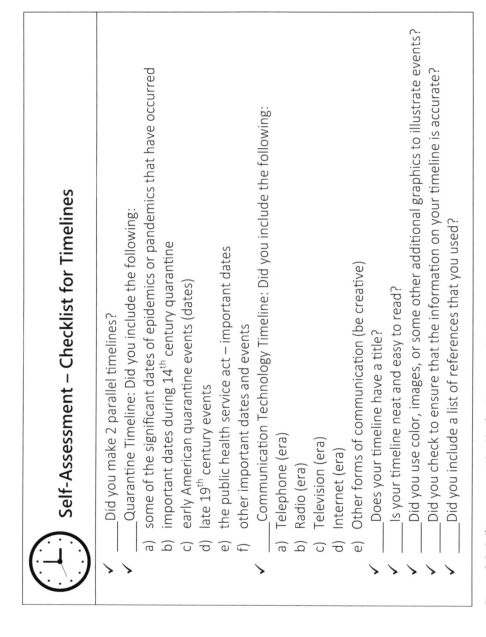

Figure 3.2 Self-Assessment: Checklist for Quarantine Timelines.

Explore

All over the world, people were helping others during the global pandemic and quarantines of 2020 (Broom, 2020). Read the following three stories of human resilience and motivation. In your small group, discuss the following questions: How is each case an example of humans helping humans? What were the characteristics or circumstances that motivated individuals in these circumstances to act? What were some of the intended outcomes of these actions? What do all three stories have in common? How are they different? How was technology used to help humans in each situation? How did the actions of individuals affect the health of communities?

Stories: Heroes of the Quarantine
Story #1: Visible Hand, Poland

During an early 2020 *coronavirus* outbreak in Poland, community members faced "forced quarantine" with strict rules about leaving the house. In response, a Facebook community called "Visible Hand" was started on March 13, 2020. The group's goal was simple: finding and offering help to individuals during the lockdown. Over 2,000 members joined the private group where members were able to ask for help or offer help to others. The rules of the online community were simple (Zulwinski, 2020): (1) be kind and polite, (2) help, rather than disturb, (3) be respectful of one another's privacy, and (4) do not discuss politics or religion. In the online community, Visible Hand, members use #helpneeded to ask for help. Some of the requests during the height of the pandemic included help finding mental health services, help designing a website for a business, help delivering food to hospitals, and more. If people had help to offer, they used the #readyhelp. Some of the serves offered included help with technology security, dog walking, help buying groceries, and more. The founders and members of the Visible Hand community demonstrated their resilience as they sought creative ways to use technology to communicate and support one another during a difficult time in history.

Story #2: Gleebooks, Australia

In 2020–2021 in Sydney, Australia, when the rates of COVID-19 infection increased, the city moved into strict lockdown measures. During a lockdown in Sydney, people were allowed to leave home for four reasons only: (1) to shop for food and other essentials, (2) to receive medical care, (3) to exercise, and (4) to work or go to school when it is not possible to work or go to school from home. These rules prevented people from enjoying the luxury of browsing in their favorite stores. As a result, many businesses suffered the loss of customers and revenue. So, although the rules prevented infections and kept people physically healthy in Sydney, they took a toll on community health.

One book shop in Sydney decided to do something to help its bibliophilic community to thrive during the lockdowns. Gleebooks is a shop dedicated to providing a rich inventory of fiction and nonfiction as well as offering literary events and services to schools. Instead of closing their doors and discontinuing services during the quarantines, they thought creatively, and found another option. During the height of the pandemic in 2020, Gleebooks saw that people needed access to literature, and they responded. They offered to deliver books by bicycle to customers who were staying home during the *coronavirus* outbreak. With four locations around the city, they could reach many customers, delivering them food for the

60   Humans and Health

brain in the form of books. For customers who lived further from a store than a bicyclist could reasonably travel, they offered deals on postage. They were committed to stay in operation and serve their book-loving community. Gleebooks learned how to adapt their practices to serve their communities and stay in business. They had passionate helpers, like Nerida Ross, a cyclist at the store, who wanted to help people "stuck" at home find ways to engage their minds through books. After all, as Nerida says, "Books are a nice way of traveling without having to go anywhere" (as cited by Broom, 2020).

Story #3: Rob Biddulph, YouTube

An artist named Rob Biddulph, an internationally renowned author and illustrator, thought about the children who were quarantined at home, unable to attend school or art classes in person. He decided to help the children and their parents by creating bi-weekly drawing classes, free and open to the public. During his YouTube classes, he teaches viewers how to draw some of the characters from his books; characters like Gregasaurus, the baby stegosaurus (Biddulph, 2020, March 16). The classes are fun and easy to follow. See Figure 3.3 for an example of a picture the author drew during Mr. Biddulph's Gregasaurus class.

On May 21, 2020, Mr. Biddulph was added to the Guinness book of world records for the largest online art class ever held (Guinness World Records, 2020); 45,611 people tuned in that day to #DrawWithRob.

Explain

One of the heroes of the quarantine, Rob Biddulph, created bi-weekly online drawing classes. For his efforts, he was recognized and received a Point of Light award from the prime minister in the United Kingdom (Biddulph, 2021). The Point of Light awards, first established by George HW Bush in the USA in 1990, recognizes individuals who make positive change in their

Figure 3.3 Gregasaurus. Drawing by the author, 2021.

communities. The Point of Light awards celebrate outstanding volunteers who are finding solutions to problems in their everyday lives, and therefore making positive, healthy change in their communities. People who receive the Point of Light designation have done something inspirational that may have helped others. They are a positive "light" in a community.

Explain Activity

1. *Draw:* Take one of Rob Biddulph's online art classes (Biddulph, 2020, March 16). Draw your own Gregasaurus. Notice how you feel before, during, and after you draw the baby dinosaur.
2. *Share:* Share your drawings with your small group.
3. *Discuss:* How did this experience make you feel? How do you think this experience might have helped kids who were scared or sick and isolated at home? Do you think that Rob Biddulph should have received the Point of Light recognition? Who do you know that is a point of life in your life? Who is a point of light in your classroom? Who is a point of light in your home? Who is a point of light in your community? Explain to your group how the people you have identified contribute to the health of the communities where they live.
4. *Recognize:* Design a certificate for one of the people that you recognized. Thank them for being a point of light in your life.

Extension Activity

As a class, consider hosting a Point of Light ceremony or breakfast, honoring all of those who you have recognized as making healthy contributions to their communities.

Think About It...

How might you volunteer in your school or in your community and become a point of light for others?

Elaborate

During the quarantines of 2020, technology was used to connect humans to one another. We also used technology to connect humans to knowledge and information. Even though many children around the world were at home and not at school, the learning never stopped. Teachers created and delivered online lesson plans in a virtual learning environment. Find a teacher at your school who taught during the global pandemic of 2020–2021. Interview them and ask them how they adapted their teaching to this new virtual model of instruction.

Talk About It...

TEACHER INTERVIEW QUESTIONS

1. What is your name and what do you teach?
2. What was it like teaching school in 2020–2021?

Table 3.2 Rubric for Interview Summary

Below Expectations	Approaching Expectations	Meets Expectations	Exceeds Expectations
Does not summarize interview. Errors interfere with the reader's understanding.	Summarizes parts of the interview, but lacks details. Some errors in capitalization, punctuation, and spelling.	Complete summary of the main ideas of the interview with some details. Few errors in conventions of English, but errors do not interfere with the reader's understanding.	Complete summary includes paraphrasing of main ideas and significant details from the interview. Includes one to two quotes from the teacher. Includes a topic sentence and concluding sentence. Few to no errors in conventions of the English language (correct use of capitalization, punctuation, spelling, etc.)

3. What was the most difficult thing about teaching during a quarantine?
4. What was the best thing about teaching online?
5. What did you learn?

Write About It...

Write a summary of what you learned during your interview with the teacher. Consider honoring this teacher with a Point of Light award (Table 3.2).

Evaluate

Human health is multi-faceted. When we talk about health, we often talk about what we need in order to be healthy. In 1943, a psychologist, Abraham Maslow, wrote a paper discussing the hierarchy of human needs. The basic needs of food, water, and shelter come first and are the most essential for survival. These are our physiological needs. Other basic needs include the need to feel safe and secure. Following our physiological needs come our social needs. Humans need to feel that they are loved and that they belong to a human group. We need friends and community. During a quarantine, the isolation protects some of our physiological needs while neglecting some of our social needs. This is why many people struggle with prolonged, worldwide quarantines during a global pandemic. However, as we have seen during this project, humans continue to find ways to adapt and stay healthy. Humans find ways to stay connected during times of isolation. Whether through a social media platform like Facebook, through online classes from a local teacher or internationally renowned author/illustrator, or through delivery services, people find ways to help one another survive and thrive during difficult and uncertain times. Part of the reason for this is that humans are resilient. For the evaluation stage of this project, define the term *resilient*. Create a poster or digital display of ways that humans demonstrated a spirit of resilience during the global pandemic of 2020–2021. Use examples from this text or research additional stories for this project.

Additional Resources

1. Listen to this one-minute National Public Radio story about the nightly salute to health care workers in New York City (Hardcastle, G., 2020, April 10). Go here for the audio file and transcript: https://www.npr.org/transcripts/832131816
2. Watch one of the YouTube videos produced by Mo Willems called "Lunch doodles with Mo!" Go here to see Episode 1 and draw: https://youtu.be/RmzjCPQv3y8

> **A Note to Teachers**: Resilience is critical for surviving and thriving after trauma or secondary traumatic stress. There are many resources for you as you support your students in developing resilience (Cahill et al., 2014). Moreover, there are many resources available for you as you develop resilience in your life as a professional educator. Some of the important factors for resiliency in both students and teachers include: finding a sense of meaning and purpose, developing self-awareness, finding emotional support, practicing healthy coping mechanisms, using humor, positive thinking, and the ability to adapt to change.

Project #5: Peace and Human Health

Academic Learning Objectives

Students will:

a) Read and analyze excerpts from famous historical primary source documents.
b) Define the term peace and explain how peace contributes to physical, social, emotional, and mental health.
c) Represent the concept of peace with a creative visual display. Present the display to the class by presenting answers to the Project #5 essential questions.
d) Read, analyze, and summarize in your own words two articles from the Treaty of Guadalupe Hidalgo.
e) Write a letter to a leader asking for peace.
f) Write and deliver a 2021 version of a chance for peace speech for a local community.

SEL Competencies

a) **Self-awareness:** As students strive to understand the complex concept of peace, they will learn how to identify their emotions and how their emotions influence their behavior.
b) **Self-management:** Students will explore ways to set collective goals about creating peaceful environments and use personal agency towards meeting these goals.
c) **Social awareness:** Students will understand the perspectives of people who live in other countries of the world as they work toward finding peaceful solutions to conflict. They will recognize when historical or current situations require peace-keeping individuals or collective peace-keeping strategies.
d) **Relationship skills:** Students will observe how online communities are using relationships to promote cross-cultural communication, understandings, and peace.
e) **Responsible decision-making:** Students will reflect on their role in peace-making in their communities, classrooms, and homes.

Essential Questions

1. What does peace mean to you?
2. What is the relationship of peace to physical, social, emotional, and mental health?
3. Do you believe that all humanity shares the common hunger for peace, fellowship, and justice?
4. How are humans creatively using technology to promote peace?
5. What is the role of peace in community health?

Stages of Inquiry

Introduction to the Problem

On April 16, 1953, President Eisenhower gave his famous "Chance for Peace" speech to the American society of newspaper editors at their luncheon at the Hotel Statler in Washington DC. In this speech, he discusses five ways that the United States has chosen to conduct its foreign affairs. One is with the belief that no people can be held as an enemy because "all humanity shares the common hunger for peace and fellowship and justice" (Eisenhower, 1953). In this project, students will explore the concepts of peace, humanity, and justice as they relate to individual and community health. In particular, students will look at how humans are using technology as a method for building and keeping peace on earth.

Engage

When Eisenhower gave his 1953 speech, "Chance for Peace" (see Figure 3.4), the world was at a critical juncture. This speech was given near the end of the Korean War, only eight years after the end of WWII. The need for peace in the world was paramount. In the speech, he

HOLD FOR RELEASE   HOLD FOR RELEASE   HOLD FOR RELEASE

April 16, 1953

CONFIDENTIAL: The following address by the President, to be delivered at the luncheon of the American Society of Newspaper Editors in the Hotel Statler, April 16, 1953, is to be held in strict confidence and no portion, synopsis or intimation is to be given out or published until actual delivery of the address. Delivery is scheduled for 1:00 p.m. EST. Extreme care must be exercised to avoid premature publication.

JAMES C. HAGERTY, PRESS SECRETARY TO THE PRESIDENT

---

① — a just peace

In this spring of 1953, the free world weighs one question above all others: the chances for a just peace for all peoples.

To weigh this chance is to summon instantly to mind another recent moment of great decision. It came with that yet more hopeful spring of 1945, bright with the promise of victory and of freedom. The hopes of all just men in *that* moment, too, was a just and lasting peace.

The eight years that have passed have seen that hope waver(s) and grow dim, and almost die. And the shadow of fear again has darkly lengthened across the world.

Today the hope of free men remains stubborn and brave, but it is sternly disciplined by experience.

It shuns not only all crude counsel of despair, but also the self-deceit of easy illusion.

It weighs the chance for peace with sure, clear knowledge of what happened to the vain hopes of 1945.

In that spring of victory, the soldiers of the Western Allies met the soldiers of Russia in the center of Europe. They were triumphant comrades in arms. Their peoples shared the joyous prospect of building, in honor of their dead, the only fitting monument -- an age of just peace.

All these war-weary peoples shared, too, this concrete, decent purpose: to guard vigilantly against the domination ever again of any part of the world by a single, unbridled aggressive power.

This common purpose lasted an instant -- and perished. The nations of the world divided to follow two distinct roads.

The United States and our valued friends, the other free nations, chose one road.

The leaders of the Soviet Union chose another.

The way chosen by the United States was plainly marked by a few clear precepts which govern its conduct in world affairs.

First: No people on earth can be held -- as a *people* -- to be an enemy, for all humanity shares the common hunger for peace and fellowship and justice.

Second: No nation's security and well-being can be lastingly achieved in isolation, but only in effective cooperation with fellow-nations.

Third: (Any) Every nation's right to a form of government and an economic system of its own choosing is *inalienable*.

Fourth: Any nation's attempt to dictate to other nations their form of government is *indefensible*.

more

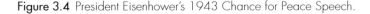

Figure 3.4 President Eisenhower's 1943 Chance for Peace Speech.

recognizes the power of the United States and the Soviet Union. He distinguishes between the two "distinct roads" that each nation has chosen to travel. The road of the United States is one guided by five precepts, or general rules. The first precepts are as follows (Eisenhower, 1953):

> First: No people on earth can be held – as a people – to be an enemy, for all humanity shares the common hunger for peace and fellowship and justice.
> Second: No nation's security and well-being can be lastingly achieved in isolation, but only in effective cooperation with fellow-nations.

Engage Activity

With your small group, discuss the following:

1. What is peace? Is the definition the same for an individual and a community? For example, what does peace look like for you, personally? What does it look like in your classroom?
2. How do we achieve peace? Personally? In our classrooms? In our communities? In our country? In the world?
3. Do you agree that all humanity shares the common hunger for peace and fellowship and justice?
4. Read the second precept: Do you agree or disagree with this idea? Justify your response.
5. What is the relationship between peace and health?

Explore

Often, when we think about peace, we think about the opposite of war. However, the concept of peace is more complicated than merely the absence of hostility or fighting. Leaders throughout history have tried to promote peace through written agreements called peace treaties. Peace treaties usually contain articles or rules for peaceful interactions between groups. Many times, these articles describe the boundaries or absence of certain types of hostile behaviors. However, peace is more than the absence of something. To have peace or to be peaceful, there must be something that replaces the violence or negativity that once existed during a time of non-peace. Peace can be a characteristic of a relationship between two individuals, communities, or nations. Peace can also be a state of being within oneself. Therefore, to really know peace, both social awareness and self-awareness are needed.

Katz (2020) describes peace as being elusive; that is, it is very difficult to describe, define, and understand in simple terms. Unlike war, which may be easier to recognize and therefore concretely define, peace is more abstract. However, it is important to try to understand and achieve peace, as humans have been doing forever. Katz talks about peace as special moments that are important to provide hope for a better future. He also talks about peace and communication. In particular, he describes how peacekeeping individuals are using digital

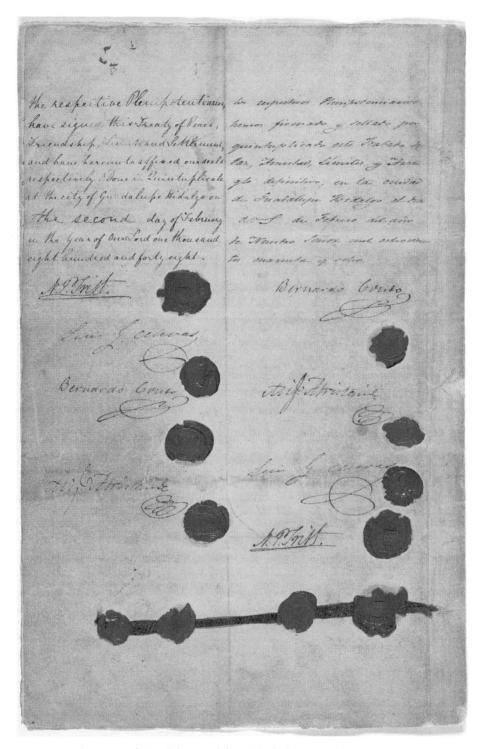

Figure 3.5 The Treaty of Guadalupe Hidalgo (1848) Signature Page.

communities to promote peace and understanding. These modern approaches to peace are exciting. However, before studying how we can use social media technologies to promote peace, let's look at how leaders communicated and negotiated the idea of peace historically, using written documents called treaties (Figure 3.5).

The Treaty of Guadalupe Hidalgo (1848)

The Treaty of Guadalupe Hidalgo ended the two-year-long Mexican–American War which began on May 13, 1846. This was a war that the United States declared against Mexico, as the United States sought western expansion. President James K. Polk was unrelenting in his pursuit of Manifest Destiny, the belief that American settlers were destined to expand and claim the land from coast to coast. The irony of this peace treaty is that there was peace before the war. But, the more powerful nation, hungry for even more power and land acquisition, would not settle for the status quo. So, after the short war, when the powerful United States was successful in the pursuit of land, new borders had to be established and a peaceful relationship between the neighboring countries had to be renegotiated.

The Treaty of Guadalupe Hidalgo is the document that leaders used to outline the desired outcomes.

The purpose of The Treaty of Guadalupe Hidalgo (1848) is to "establish upon a solid basis relations of peace and friendship, which shall confer reciprocal benefits upon the citizens of both, and assure the concord, harmony, and mutual confidence wherein the two peoples should live, as good neighbors." There are five articles in the treaty of Guadalupe Hidalgo.

Explore Activity

Explore articles from the Treaty of Guadalupe Hidalgo. Read and analyze Article 1 and an excerpt from Article 5. Based on your understanding of the readings, what can you conclude about the purpose of the treaty. Write a summary of each article in your own words, including any inferences that you made (Table 3.3).

Table 3.3 Rubric for Summary of Article 1 and Article 5 of the Treaty of Guadalupe Hidalgo

Below Expectations	Approaching Expectations	Meets Expectations	Exceeds Expectations
The student did not write a summary of both articles in their own words. They restated each article or misinterpreted the meaning. The conventions of English, including spelling, capitalization, word choice, and punctuation interfere with meaning.	The student wrote a summary of both articles, with some correct interpretations of meaning. No inferences were included. There were some errors in spelling, capitalization, word choice, and punctuation that require revision.	The student wrote a summary of each article in their own words, correctly interpreting the meaning. The student drew one inference based on their reading. Good use of the conventions of English.	The student wrote a summary of each article in their own words, correctly interpreting the meaning. They conveyed the main idea of each article and gave a supporting example. They drew some inferences based on their summaries. Excellent use of conventions of English.

Article 1: There shall be firm and universal peace between the United States of America and the Mexican Republic, and between their respective countries, territories, cities, towns, and people, without exception of places or persons.

Article 5: The boundary line between the two Republics shall commence in the Gulf of Mexico, three leagues from land, opposite the mouth of the Rio Grande, otherwise called Rio Bravo del Norte,…from thence up the middle of that river, following the deepest channel, where it has more than one, to the point where it strikes the southern boundary of New Mexico; thence, westwardly, along the whole southern boundary of New Mexico (which runs north of the town called Paso) to its western termination; thence, northward, along the western line of New Mexico, until it intersects the first branch of the river Gila;…thence down the middle of the said branch and of the said river, until it empties into the Rio Colorado; thence across the Rio Colorado, following the division line between Upper and Lower California, to the Pacific Ocean. And, in order to preclude all difficulty in tracing upon the ground the limit separating Upper from Lower California, it is agreed that the said limit shall consist of a straight line drawn from the middle of the Rio Gila, where it unites with the Colorado, to a point on the coast of the Pacific Ocean, distant one marine league due south of the southernmost point of the port of San Diego, according to the plan of said port made in the year 1782 by Don Juan Pantoja.

Results of the Treaty

There were many results of the treaty; but one of the most striking is the amount of land that Mexico ceded to the United States, resulting in a large territorial expansion of the United States including areas that include modern-day Texas, Colorado, Arizona, Utah, California, and Nevada. Mexico also gave up all claims to Texas and agreed on the Rio Grande as the border.

Class Discussion Questions

1. What are some of the lasting effects of this peace treaty for Americans living in the southwest United States?
2. What are some of the lasting effects of this peace treaty for Mexican citizens?
3. Do you think that this treaty *or* any treaty affects both sides in the same way?
4. Is it possible for any peace agreement to be completely fair? What affects the "fairness" of an agreement?
5. How important is fairness or justice for people's mental, social, and emotional health?

A Note to Teachers: Help students explore the role of power in negotiations. Power may tip the scales of fairness. Help students understand why it is important for the person with power to be compassionate and empathetic, and how leveling the power differential might benefit everyone who is striving for peace and healthy relationships. If necessary, give students an additional opportunity to dialog around the complicated issues of power, fairness, peace, and healthy relationships.

Explain

Now that you have spent some time thinking about peace, create a visual display of your understanding of peace. This could be a digital infographic, hand-drawn image or symbol, a collage, a painting, a sculpture, or anything else that you think will represent your ideas about peace. You may use any tools or materials available to create your display. Be creative. Be prepared to share your display and discuss how it relates to individual and community health. Use resources from this chapter or from your own research to support the development of your ideas. The discussion of your display should address the following essential questions: What does peace mean to you? What is the relationship of peace to physical, social, emotional, and mental health? Do you believe that all humanity shares the common hunger for peace, fellowship, and justice? How are humans creatively using technology to promote peace? What is the role of peace in community health (Figure 3.6)?

Elaborate

In the year 2021, we are no longer left to wonder what people in other parts of the world think about peace. Using digital platforms and social media, we can ask them. With the touch of a screen, we can connect with peacekeeping people from all over the world. Using technology, we can learn how to live more peacefully with one another. Katz (2020) says that there are four ways that technology can help us achieve peace:

1. **Play** – we can use technology to learn how to live peacefully by playing games that simulate peace. One example is an experience called the World Peace Game (Hunter, 2021). The mission of the World Peace Game is to help children understand that peace isn't just idea, it is an achievable goal that we can work toward. While playing, students learn the strategies for resolving conflicts and finding compromise. The World Peace Game is a game that can be incorporated into classrooms and schools.
2. **Explore** – there are many websites that allow us to see what peace looks like in various parts of the world. One example is the global peace index which gives

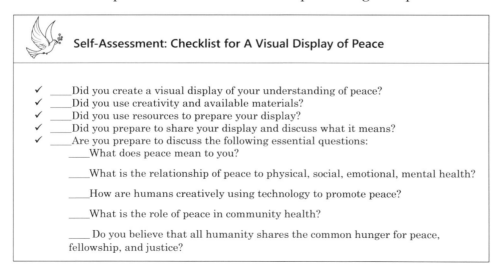

Figure 3.6 Self-Assessment: Checklist for A Visual Display of Peace.

Humans and Health 71

countries a rating based on 23 indicators. The country is rated on a scale of 1–5. The lower the score, the more peaceful the country. At the time of this writing (June 6, 2021), the country with the lowest, most peaceful rating was Iceland (Vision of Humanity, 2021).

3. **Listen** – blogs and online social media communities have become places and spaces for promoting peace through messaging and storytelling (Peace Direct, 2020). It is in these digital spaces that people can listen and learn from others who care about peace. It is also in these spaces that people can hear from those who are living in areas of the world experiencing conflict and war.

4. **Participate** – finally, there are many ways that future peacekeepers, like you, can get involved in peacemaking communities and processes. For example, the organization Kids for Peace invites kids to participate in acts of kindness and acts of service with global partners (Kids for Peace, 2017). They also have a peace pledge program and racial justice resources for educators and families. Other ways that youth can participate in promoting peace is to ask for it directly. This can be done through letters or emails sent directly to decision-makers and leaders charged with keeping the peace in your communities. This is exactly what Pam Kaplan did when she wrote a letter to President Nixon asking for peace (see Figure 3.7).

Elaborate Activity

Write a letter or message to a leader in your community asking them to promote peace. This could be a leader in your school, church, home, state, or country. Work with your teacher or parent and use technology to send your letter or message. This could be in the form of an email or direct message using a social media platform. Ensure that you get your parents' permission before completing this assignment.

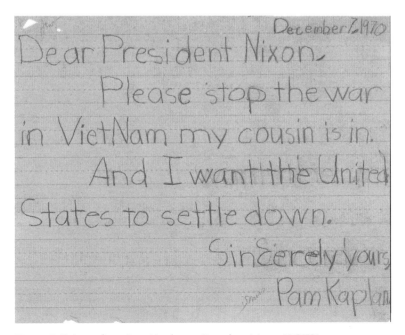

Figure 3.7 Letter from Pam Kaplan to President Nixon (1970).

Evaluate

Write Your Own: Chance for Peace Speech – The 2021 Version

What is a community that you know that needs to give peace a chance? Maybe it is in your home, or in your classroom. Maybe it is a conflict you learned about that is happening in another country. Identify a community. Write a 3–5-minute speech that you will give to your class that addresses the community. In your speech, introduce the community and the issue. What is the conflict or why isn't there peace at the moment? Next, identify two precepts, ground rules, that you want the community to follow. Then, list three to five behaviors that would promote peace in this community. Finally, conclude your speech with a strong statement about the health benefits of peace for the individual and the community as a whole. Practice your speech. Review the Rubric for the Change for Peace Oral Presentation to ensure that you are meeting expectations in the following areas: presentation of knowledge and oral communication skills. See Table 3.4.

Project #6: Healing and Art

Academic Learning Objectives

Students will:

a) Explain the importance of healing for individual and community health.
b) Describe and compare various examples and processes of healing such as physical healing, emotional healing, and community healing.
c) Analyze art and interpret artist's intent. Determine if art may be used for healing. Define art therapy.
d) Collaborate with a team to organize artistic ideas that relate to personal experience and create a community artwork: a healing mural or sculpture.
e) Write a personal narrative about a time when you healed. Use this narrative as inspiration to create a sculpture or painting that represents your experience.

SEL Competencies

a) **Responsible decision-making:** Students will practice curiosity and open-mindedness as they analyze art and interpret intended meaning. They will think critically as they compare types and processes of healing. They will evaluate how a collaborative community project might impact community culture and well-being.
b) **Relationship skills:** Students will collaborate with a team to create a community artwork, a mural. They will practice communicating effectively, problem-solving, resolving conflict, and leadership.

Table 3.4 Rubric for the Chance for Peace Oral Presentation

Category	Below Expectations	Approaching Expectations	Meets Expectations	Exceeds Expectations
Presentation of knowledge and ideas	Student is not prepared to present ideas, is unorganized, or missing most elements.	Speech includes some of the required elements. There is an attempt to organize ideas, but revision is necessary.	Speech is organized. All required elements of the speech are included including identifying the community, discussing the problem, stating two precepts, three to five behaviors, and a concluding statement.	Student uses a story or quote to get our attention. Speech is organized. All required elements of the speech are included including identifying the community, discussing the problem, stating two precepts, three to five behaviors, and a strong concluding statement. Speech is three to five minutes in length.
Oral communication skills	Speech is unclear and/or too loud or soft. No eye contact or gestures. No preparation is apparent.	Speech is occasionally unclear and volume is sometimes inappropriate. Somewhat maintains attention of the audience with eye contact. It is unclear as to whether the student prepared for the speech.	Speech is clear and volume is appropriate. Maintains attention of the audience with eye contact. Student obviously prepared for the speech.	Speech is clear and volume is appropriate. Maintains attention of the audience with eye contact and helpful gestures. Uses voice to emphasize key points. Engages audience with non-verbal and verbal communication. Student obviously prepared for the speech.
Style and attitudes (SEL competencies)	Lacks understanding of personal strengths and the importance of peace.	Communicates values and attitudes about the importance of peace only.	Engaging style. Communicates values and attitudes about the importance of peace.	Engaging personal style. Capitalizes on own strengths. Communicates values and attitudes about the importance of peace. Demonstrates care for others' individual and community health.

Essential Questions

1. What can hurt an individual? What can hurt a community?
2. How can people heal: individually and as communities?
3. Can humans use art to heal?
4. How is physical healing similar or different to community healing?

Stages of Inquiry
Introduction to the Problem

What happens when you get hurt? Think about a time when you got a scratch or a simple injury that broke the surface of your skin. It probably hurt. Maybe the skin became red and swollen. Perhaps you even bled a little bit, but then the bleeding stopped and, over time, you healed. The human body has remarkable mechanisms for healing. In fact, there are several lines of defense that can protect and heal you when you get injured or sick, because we all get hurt sometimes.

There are other ways that people can be hurt. We can hurt emotionally when someone doesn't recognize our perspective or consider our strengths. Our feelings can be hurt when we find ourselves in unjust situations. We can have mental illness too, which can hurt us psychologically and sometimes physically too. People get hurt sometimes; but we heal too.

Similarly, communities can hurt sometimes too. We can hurt as communities when we fail to cooperate and collaborate to solve our collective problems. There are times when people in a community may disagree. Other times, a community may face a shared tragedy. There are times when, collectively, we are sad, confused, hurt, or afraid. When this happens, communities need to heal too.

Engage

Thanks to science, we know how human bodies heal, but how do communities heal? One hypothesis that is being tested in communities around the world is that art can heal. In Louisville, Kentucky, Project HEAL (Health, Equity, Art, Learning) tested the hypothesis: *Art can heal communities*. Project HEAL is a community development project that uses art and cultural projects to increase civic engagement and health equity. At Project HEAL, they believe that art and artists can do four things to promote healing in communities (Robert Wood Johnson Foundation (RWJF), 2017):

1. They believe that artists can "create opportunities for a shared vision of a healthier, more connected future" (RWJF, 2017). By giving voice to members of communities who may typically feel left out, they can begin conversations about what people need and how to improve conditions for them. More than anything, these conversations bring hope. And, as they say, "hope heals."
2. The second thing that artists and art can do for communities is bring neighbors together and give them tools for facing and addressing adversity. When

something sad happens, creating art together helps people process emotions, grieve, and heal.
3. Art can be used to facilitate dialogue with policymakers. Art provides visual imagery that helps people understand and talk about difficult issues.
4. Shared art provides a shared experience, builds bridges, and connects people who may not have found common ground prior to creating the art. Therefore, the experience of making art together can pioneer new relationships.

Engage Activity

As part of project HEAL, an artist, Andrew Cozzens, created a sculpture entitled: "Smoketown Life | Line Project" (Cozzens, 2017).

Let's spend some time looking at and analyzing this artwork. View the artwork on the artist's website here: https://www.andrewcozzens.com/white-dreams-collection

Before you read the description, let's use a three-step process to analyze this work. Discuss your ideas with your group.

1. **Observe** – what do you see? Be specific. Look at the small details and the big picture. Notice the colors, shapes, textures, materials, etc.
2. **Think (interpret)** – based on what you see, what do you think about? What do you think the artist was thinking when he made this sculpture? What do you think he was trying to say through this artwork?
3. **Wonder** – how do you think this piece might connect with what is going on in the world today? What does it make you wonder about or imagine?

> **EXTENSION ACTIVITY (FOR TEACHERS ONLY)**
>
> The Smoketown Life | Line Project Sculpture has deep meanings and significance to the lives in Smoketown. Read the artist's explanation of how his works enable us to visualize the trauma of individuals in this community. His intention is for the project to be used to ask questions and find solutions to help the residents of this community. Ask yourself how his art might be used for policy changes that will improve individual and community health.

Explore

Healing is a complicated, multi-step process. Let's explore the non-specific defense mechanism in the human body that initiates healing when a small, physical hurt occurs. Your body is equipped with a system that protects you from the hurt caused by getting sick or injured. This system can also heal you when you do get hurt or sick. In this system, there are several lines of defense. The first line of defense is your skin. Your skin keeps the bad germs like bacteria and viruses out. Your skin is amazing! It is made of epithelial tissue which is in layers. It is waterproof, so you don't leak! It has so many sensory cells so that you can feel and react to external stimuli like heat, cold, and pain. The skin and the membranes in your nose and mouth are the first line of defense. You have other defense cells inside your body that can gobble up any foreign invaders that get past the first barrier. These cells called phagocytes are important warriors in your body's ability to protect and heal. When your skin is damaged, the body activates an important healing process called the inflammatory response (Reece, 2014).

The inflammatory response is the process that your body uses to heal you when your puppy dog accidentally nips your heels or when you fall and skin your knee on the playground.

The inflammatory response works like this: You get a small injury. Your skin tissue is damaged. Bacteria and other germs get past your skin and into your body. Your body responds by releasing chemical signals that cause tiny blood vessels called capillaries to open up and become permeable. This allows blood to flow to the area. Inside your blood, special cells called platelets stop the bleeding. White blood cells called phagocytes engulf (eat) any of the bacteria or other germs that entered at the site of the injury. Since more blood is flowing to the injured area, it might look red and swollen for a while. Eventually, the clotting blood and dead germs will form pus and a scab. Sometimes, you may even get a scar. But, all of that is good because it means that you are healing. The body has a way to heal itself.

> *Key terms:* injury, bacteria, germs, capillaries, platelets, phagocytes, inflammatory response

The body can heal itself from simple cuts and scrapes and from more serious illnesses like certain viruses that infiltrate deeper into our bodies' systems. When a more intricate, specific plan for healing is needed, the immune system's specific response is activated. There are wonderful cells called T-cells and B-cells that work together to heal you. It is a complicated, beautiful process that, when effective, keeps us healthy!

Explore Activity

Create a drawing that illustrates how your body heals a scraped knee using the inflammatory response. Include a title and label your drawing (Table 3.5).

Explain

In the past few years, we have seen the creation of art in response to hurtful events in communities. We have seen murals on downtown buildings, on city streets, and in public spaces. In some cases, this is participatory art in which all community members are invited to join in the creation. Other times, a commissioned artist creates and installs the work for all to enjoy. In both cases, these artworks can be sources of hope, inspiration, and health. Hospitals are even installing art displays, noting the powerful healing properties of these spaces for patients and their families.

One of these projects from the Arts in Medicine program at MD Anderson, Cancer Center was a collaborative community project to create a large-scale dragon sculpture out of paper, entitled "Okoa the Wave Rider."

Table 3.5 Rubric for Scientific Illustration – The Inflammatory Response

Below Expectations	**Approaching Expectations**	**Meets Expectations**	**Exceeds Expectations**
The student omits some steps or body parts involved in the inflammatory response. There are no labels, no title, and little effort was made to represent the scientific concept.	The student includes some steps or body parts involved in the inflammatory response. There are some labels and some effort was made to represent the scientific concept.	Student's drawing includes all of the significant steps and parts of the body involved in the inflammatory response. The drawing has a title and labels. The student was neat. The drawing represents the scientific concepts.	Student's drawing includes all of the significant steps and parts of the body involved in the inflammatory response. The drawing has a title, labels, and is colored. The student was neat and precise and the drawing represents the scientific concepts well.

Watch a video on YouTube (2014) called: "How a Monstrous Art Project Brought Cancer Patients Together" here: https://youtu.be/cElSsKvNIR4

Explain Activity

Once you have seen and heard about the community sculpture project at MD Anderson, explain to your partner how the creation of the sculpture helped to provide healing to the community. Share your understandings about the different kinds of healing that exist, and take turns explaining the answers to the following essential questions: What can hurt an individual? What can hurt a community? How can people heal: individually and as communities? Can humans use art to heal? How is physical healing similar to or different from community healing?

Elaborate

Writing Prompt: For this phase of the project, you will spend some time reflecting on a time when you needed healing, and healed. Think about how you were hurt. Did a friend hurt your feelings? Did you break your leg playing soccer? What happened? How did it happen? Who helped you? What did you need to do so that you would heal? How do you feel about what happened? Discuss your thoughts and feelings. Write a personal narrative telling us the story of a time of healing. Use significant details to share your memory. If necessary, include dialogue. Illustrate your story with descriptive language, so that you are showing, more than telling, what happened. Focus on the process of healing in the narrative. Make sure to organize your thoughts in paragraphs. Include a beginning, middle, and end to the story. Refer to Figure 2.5 to review the writing cycle. Make sure to brainstorm ideas and prewrite, write, revise, edit, rewrite, and submit a publishable final product (Table 3.6).

Table 3.6 Rubric for Narrative Writing Assignment – A Time of Healing

Below Expectations	**Approaching Expectations**	**Meets Expectations**	**Exceeds Expectations**
The author answers the questions in the writing prompt, but does not connect the ideas in a narrative story. Details are lacking and connections to big ideas are omitted.	Author writes about a time when they healed. The author addresses some of the writing prompt but omits important details or lacks connection to the big ideas of a healing process.	Narrative story is about a time when the author healed. The author shares a memory using descriptive language and some details. The author talks about what they learned about the process of healing. There is a beginning, middle, and end.	Narrative story is about a time when the author healed. Significant details and memories are shared. The author uses examples or dialogue. Descriptive language illustrates the event clearly. The author connects the event to what they have learned about the process of healing. There is a beginning, middle, and end to the story. The story is organized in paragraphs.

Evaluate

In this project, we learned about healing and art. In your small groups, review the processes of healing for individuals and communities. As the final stage of inquiry in this project, brainstorm some of the issues that you believe are currently hurting communities in America. Discuss how collaborative art could be used to bring people together and heal these communities.

Extension Activity

Class Project: Identify an issue that your classroom community has faced this year. Design a community artwork to express your collective feelings about the issue. Work together to plan and create this art. Consider creating a large mural or sculpture that will promote peace, healing, and health.

Bibliography

Anderson, M.D. (2014, Sept. 2). How a Monstrous Art Project Brought Cancer Patients Together. Retrieved on August 1, 2021 from https://youtu.be/cElSsKvNIR4

Biddulf, R. (2020, March 16). #DrawWithRob 1 Gregasaurus [Video]. YouTube. Retrieved on August 1, 2021 from https://youtu.be/bhyCxVPb1qU

Biddulph, R. (2021). Who on Earth is Rob Biddulph? [website]. Retrieved on August 1, 2021 from http://www.robbiddulph.com/about

Broom, D. (2020). Meet the Everyday Heroes of the Pandemic. World Economic Forum. Retrieved on July 31, 2021 from https://www.weforum.org/agenda/2020/03/meet-the-everyday-heroes-of-the-covid-19-crisis/

Cahill, H., Beadle, S., Farrelly, A., Forster, R., & Smith, K. (2014). Building Resilience in Children and Young People: *A Literature Review for the Department of Education and Early Childhood Development* (DEECD). Melbourne, Victoria: Department of Education, Victoria.

Cozzens, A. (2017). "Smoketown Life | Line Project" White-dreams Collection. [photograph of artwork]. Retrieved on July 31, 2021 from https://www.andrewcozzens.com/white-dreams-collection

Eisenhower, D.D. (1953, April 16). "Chance for Peace" Speech. American Society News – paper Editors Reading Copy; Papers as President of the United States; Dwight D. Eisenhower Library, Abilene, KS. Retrieved on October 25, 2021 from https://www.docsteach.org/documents/document/chance-for-peace-speech

Gleebooks. (2020). About Gleebooks. Retrieved on June 1, 2021 from https://www.gleebooks.com.au/about/.

Guinness World Records. (2020, June 8). Children's Illustrator Rob Biddulph Leads Record-breaking Art Lesson. Retrieved on June 1, 2021 from https://www.guinnessworldrecords.com/news/2020/6/childrens-illustrator-rob-biddulph-leads-record-breaking-art-lesson-620354

Hardcastle, G. (2020, April 10). *Every Night, New York City Salutes Its Health Care Workers*. NPR. All Things Considered. Retrieved on October 25, 2021 from https://www.npr.org/2020/04/10/832131816/every-night-new-york-city-salutes-its-health-care-workers

History of Quarantine. (2020). Centers for Disease Control and Prevention, Centers for Disease Control and Prevention, 20 July 2020, Retrieved on February 15, 2021 from www.cdc.gov/quarantine/historyquarantine.html

Hunter, J. (2021). World Peace Game – Mission and Approach. [webpage] Retrieved on July 1, 2021 from https://worldpeacegame.org/the-game/mission/

Katz, Y. (2020). Interacting for Peace: Re-thinking Peace through Digital Platforms. *Social Media + Society*, 6(2), 1–11. https://doi.org/10.1177%2F2056305120926620

Kids for Peace. (2017). Kids for Peace: Uplifting Our World Through Peace and Action. [website]. Retrieved on May 15, 2021 from https://kidsforpeaceglobal.org.

Letter from Pam Kaplan to President Nixon and White House Response; 12/7/1970; White House Alpha (Alphabetical) Name Files, 1/20/1969 – 8/9/1974; Collection RN-WHAN: White House Alpha (Alphabetical) Name Files (Nixon Administration); Richard Nixon Library, Yorba Linda, CA. [Online Version, https://www.docsteach.org/documents/document/a-childs-request, July 31, 2021].

Maslow, A.H. (1943). A Theory of Human Motivation. *Psychological Review*, 50(4), 370–396. https://doi.org/10.1037/h0054346

National Core Art Standards. (2021). Home | National Core Arts Standards (nationalartsstandards.org)

National Governors Association Center for Best Practices, Council of Chief State School Officers. (2010). *Common Core State Standards (Insert Specific Content Area If You Are Using Only One)*. Washington D.C.: Author. Retrieved on August 1, 2021 from http://corestandards.org/

National Health Education Standards. (2019). National Health Education Standards - SHER | Healthy Schools | CDC. Retrieved on August 1, 2021 from https://www.cdc.gov/healthyschools/sher/standards/index.htm

NGSS Lead States. (2013). Next Generation Science Standards: For States, by States. Retrieved on August 1, 2021 from http://www.nextgenscience.org

Peace Direct. (2020, April 6). Digital Pathways for Peace: Insights and Lessons from a Global Online Consultation [online report]. Retrieved on May 15, 2021 from https://www.peacedirect.org/us/publications/digital-pathways-for-peace/

Preamble to the Constitution of the World Health Organization as adopted by the International Health Conference, New York: World Health Organization, 19–22 June, 1946. Retrieved on March 21, 2017 from http://www.who.int/suggestions/faq/en/

President Eisenhower's "Chance for Peace" Speech; 4/16/1953; Speech 4/16/53 American Society Newspaper Editors Reading Copy; Speech Files, 1953–1961; Collection DDE-EPRES: Eisenhower, Dwight D.: Papers as President of the United States; Dwight D. Eisenhower Library, Abilene, KS. [Online Version, Retrieved on October 25, 2021 from https://www.docsteach.org/documents/document/chance-for-peace-speech, July 31, 2021]

Quarantine. (2021). In *Merriam-Webster.com*. Retrieved on May 8, 2021, from https://www.merriamwebster.com/dictionary/quarantine

Reece, J.B., Urry, L.A., Cain, M.L., Wasserman, S.A., Minorsky, P.V., Jackson, & Campbell, N.A. (2014). *Campbell Biology* (10th edition). Boston, MA: Pearson.

Robert Wood Johnson Foundation. (2017, March 2). Four Ways Artists Can Help Heal Communities. Culture of Health Blog [webpage]. Retrieved on August 1, 2021 from https://www.rwjf.org/en/blog/2017/03/four_ways_artistsca.html

Ross, N. (2020). Quote from "Meet the Everyday Heroes of the Pandemic".

Snyder, L. (1994). Passage and Significance of the 1944 Public Health Service Act. *Public Health Reports* (1974–), 109(6), 721–724. Retrieved on June 16, 2021 from http://www.jstor.org/stable/4597709

Treaty of Guadalupe Hidalgo; 2/2/1848; Perfected Treaties, 1778–1945; General Records of the United States Government, Record Group 11; National Archives Building, Washington, DC. [Online version, https://www.docsteach.org/documents/document/guadalupe-hidalgo-original, June 30, 2021]

Vision of Humanity. (2021, June 6). Maps and Data. [website] Retrieved on June 6, 2021 from https://www.visionofhumanity.org/maps/#/

Willems, M. (2020, March 16). Lunch Doodles With Mo Willems! Episode 1. [Video]. YouTube. Retrieved on July 31, 2021 from https://youtu.be/RmzjCPQv3y8.

Zulwinski, F. (2020). Visible Hand. [Facebook] March 13, 2020. Retrieved on August 1, 2021 from https://www.facebook.com/groups/2874461049277846

Chapter 4

Technology and Society

Introduction

In Chapter 4, the final set of projects, students explore the relationship between technology and society. A main theme of the final project set is scientific literacy. Scientific literacy is more than being able to read and write about science. It is the ability to process ideas using a method of analyzing data and drawing conclusions. Being scientifically literate means that you understand basic scientific concepts and the importance of applying these ideas to our real lives. Scientific literacy is about informed decision-making for healthier individuals and a healthier world (Ashbrook, 2020).

It is important for humans to have a basic understanding of scientific knowledge and concepts to evaluate the information that we encounter and to make informed decisions. On occasion, science-based decision-making can become a matter of life or death for individuals and communities. Take, for example, the decision to sit on the bank of a river watching a slow-moving snake meandering through the clear water. What kind of snake is it? Should you approach the snake, quietly observe the living organism in the environment, move slowly away from the animal, or run? Knowing a little bit about where you are in the world, and what kinds of snakes are found in the river's ecosystem can help you make an informed decision. Similarly, if you cut your finger while playing on a playground, you might need to know some basic information about the expected immune response, and first aid. Basic scientific literacy helps us to make rational and informed decisions.

Scientific literacy will also help you be a careful consumer of information. Rather than accept information at face value, a scientifically literate person can ask questions and seek evidence-based truths, rather than merely accepting popular beliefs. Scientific literacy is understanding that conclusions based on facts and evidence may differ from popular opinion. The scientific answer may not agree with the consensus (Crichton, 2003).

In this chapter, there are projects that will support students as they develop scientific literacy and skills for life-long learning. Students will be asked to explore concepts and draw their own conclusions on real-world issues based on research and analysis of data. Rather than conducting experiments in a specific scientific discipline such as biology or chemistry, students are asked to consider the importance of scientific literacy in society. These projects maintain a big picture orientation and help students begin to understand the intersection of STEAM and SEL. There is a focus on two, cross-cutting science standards throughout this chapter: (1) cause and effect and (2) the influence of engineering, science, and technology on

DOI: 10.4324/9781003247449-4

society and the natural world. There is focus on reflective writing throughout these projects. There is also emphasis on the importance of using writing to communicate and the ability to state opinions supported by reasons.

An Overview of Projects #7, #8, and #9

In Project #7, students look at a historical case study in medical technology: the development of the polio vaccine. They analyze primary source documents from the years before and after distribution of the vaccine. In this project some essential questions that they will answer include: Why is scientific literacy and a basic understanding of medical technologies important for human health? How can we use science to make responsible decisions? During this project, students are introduced to Dr. Jonas Salk, pioneer of new vaccine technologies. In this study, they will think about responsible decision-making and social awareness, reflecting on the individual's role in community well-being.

In Project #8, students will evaluate modern social media sites as sources of connection and learning. They will collect data during a self-study to answer the difficult question: Is YouTube good for me? This project is a study of self-awareness and self-management when using social media. They will consider the pros and cons of YouTube and other social media website technologies and begin to recognize the role technology plays in individual and community development. Some essential questions include: How can social media support or constrain relationship building, making human connections, and learning? What factors will motivate me to set healthy boundaries for social media consumption?

For the final project in this series, Project #9, students are encouraged to seek adventures in learning and life. They study some pioneers in land, sea, and space exploration, and evaluate some of the modern technology needed for adventure-explorers (Table 4.1).

Project #7: The Polio Vaccine

Academic Learning Objectives

Students will:

a) Use reflective writing to process how the technology that we develop today will influence future generations.
b) Explain the development of the polio vaccine and its effect on society. Develop ideas with facts, definitions, and concrete examples.
c) Reflect on your feelings about the development of the polio vaccine as a medical technology. In a written reflection, state your opinions supported by reasons.
d) Analyze and interpret visual information that supports text (maps and graphs). Draw conclusions based on your interpretations of the maps. Communicate your conclusions with a small group, supporting facts with evidence.

Technology and Society 83

Table 4.1 Overview of Projects in Chapter 4 and their alignment with Academic Standards and SEL Competencies

Project	Targeted Academic Standards for 4th–5th-Graders	Target SEL Core Competencies
7 – The Polio Vaccine	Common Core Standards CCSS.ELA-LITERACY W.4.1, W.4.4, W.4.10, W.5.1, W.5.1.C W.5.9, W.5.10 Reading – interpreting visual information R.4.7 Comprehend informational texts R.5.10 NGSS Science Cross-Cutting Standards Cause and effect Influence of engineering, science, and technology on society and the Natural World	**Social awareness:** Show concern for others **Responsible decision-making:** Recognize role in community well-being; reflect on how critical thinking skills are needed in school and society **Relationship skills:** Communicate effectively
8 – Is YouTube Good For Me?	Common Core Standards CCSS.ELA-LITERACY W.4.1, W.4.4, W.4.10, W.5.1, W.5.1.C, W.5.9, W.5.10 National Health Standards 2.5.5, 2.5.6 – Identify the role of media on health NGSS Science Cross-Cutting Standards Cause and effect Influence of engineering, science, and technology on society and the natural world	**Self-awareness:** Demonstrate honesty and integrity **Self-management:** Exhibit self-discipline and self-motivation **Relationship skills:** Communicate effectively
9 – Technology for Adventures	Common Core Standards CCSS.ELA-LITERACY W.4.1, W.4.4, W.4.10, W.5.1, W.5.1.C, W.5.9, W.5.10 National Health Standards 6.5.1, 6.5.2 – Set a healthy goal and find resources to support the goal. Make plans toward achieving the goal. NGSS Science Cross-Cutting Standards Cause and effect Influence of engineering, science, and technology on society and the natural world	**Self-awareness:** Develop interests **Responsible decision-making:** Demonstrate curiosity, accepting the consequences of one's actions **Relationship skills:** Communicating effectively

SEL Competencies

a) **Social awareness:** Using higher-order, critical thinking, students will imagine what it might have felt like to live during the time of polio in the United States. They will consider the perspectives of multiple stakeholders (parents and children). They will express concern and empathy for the challenges of this period in history.
b) **Responsible decision-making:** Recognize the role people played in community health during the development and distribution of the polio vaccine. Apply your findings to understanding your personal role in community well-being.
c) **Relationship skills:** Communicate effectively and clearly in oral and written forms.

Essential Questions

1. Why is scientific literacy and a basic understanding of medical technologies important for human health?
2. How can we use science to make responsible decisions?
3. How will the technologies we discover today influence future generations?
4. What are some examples of medical technologies that have benefitted society?
5. How do people show concern for others during times of crisis and fear?
6. How does knowledge prevent fear?

Stages of Inquiry
Introduction to the Problem
A Brief History of Polio

Poliomyelitis (polio) is a disease that is caused by a virus. Although it is likely that this disease has been around for centuries (Paul, 1971), it was not until the late 1700s that we had a medical description of the disease. In 1789, Dr. Michael Underwood described the disease as a "debility of the lower extremities." In 1894, we saw the first significant outbreak of the disease in the United States (Blume & Geesink, 2000). At the time, it was known and named for its most devastating symptom: infantile paralysis.

From the early 1900s on, we began to see significant outbreaks of this disease in Europe and in the United States. At the time we knew little about the disease. We knew even less about how it was transmitted, that is, until a Swedish physician named Ivar Wickman determined that the disease-causing agent was highly contagious, making the disease infectious (History of Vaccines, 2021).

Wickman studied the spread of the disease during an outbreak in Sweden. His most significant and frightening hypothesis was the role of asymptomatic carriers in spreading the disease. This meant that there were people without symptoms who could pass the illness to others without knowing it. In 1908, the cause of poliomyelitis was identified as poliovirus (Paul, 1971).

A virus is a non-living, disease-causing agent that needs a living cell as a host in order to survive. Like other human viruses, the poliovirus attacks and uses human cells to replicate. This process can cause humans to become sick. In this case, the poliovirus attacks motor neurons in the spinal cord and can cause paralysis, especially in children. Due to the contagious nature of the virus, we started to see polio epidemics in Europe and in the United States in the early 1900s, including a terrible outbreak in New Yok City in 1916. Polio peaked in the summer months of the 1940s and 1950s. The devastating effects of polio were visible in every town in America with children and adults becoming permanently paralyzed. Some adults and children even spent months in iron lungs, a medical technology of the 1950s that helped people who had polio to breathe and survive. Some lost their lives. It was a scary time, and scientists raced to find a solution to this global problem (Figure 4.1).

Engage

In the 1940s and 1950s, polio was rampant. There was so much that we did not know about it. Lack of knowledge can cause fear. Polio was particularly terrifying for parents in the United States and around the world. Since children seemed to be some of the people who were hit the hardest, with muscle weakness and paralysis, towns would sometimes close their schools, pools, and movie theaters during an outbreak to prevent the spread.

One particularly scary thing about poliovirus is that most people who had it were asymptomatic, meaning they did not look or sound sick. However, as Wickman hypothesized many years before, even when people were asymptomatic, they could still spread the disease. Before 1952, much was unknown about how to prevent infection.

The good news is that because of science, today, in 2021, polio is nearly eradicated (PEI, 2021). There has not been a natural polio case in the United States since 1979. In fact, it is nearly eliminated in all countries of the world. In the last few countries where polio remains, people are working hard to make sure that all children receive the vaccine. Check out the map at Polio Now on the Polio Global Eradication Initiative Website to see where in the world polio is still an issue. Go here: https://polioeradication.org/polio-today/polio-now/

Figure 4.1 Nurses Being Trained on the Use of the Iron Lung as a Treatment for Polio Victims.

Engage Activity: Class Discussion Questions

In a large group, discuss the following questions. Practice listening to the ideas and thoughts of your classmates. Contribute to the conversation by validating their ideas and adding your own opinions with reasons to support what you say (Table 4.2).

1. Why is it important to know how a disease spreads?
2. Imagine how parents in the early 1900s felt about a disease with an unknown mode of transmission. How do you think they felt? What would you have done as a parent at the time of an outbreak in your town?
3. Imagine the life of a family during a polio epidemic in the 1940s. How do you think the parents felt when they learned about another outbreak? How did the children feel when their parents told them that they could not go to the swimming pool or the movie theater?
4. How does knowledge prevent fear?
5. How do you feel about learning the good news of the near eradication of polio?

Explore
The Polio Vaccine

The polio disease, poliomyelitis and the poliovirus, are nearly eradicated in the world. The reason that we no longer close schools and pools because of polio is due to the fact that we have a vaccine. In 1953, Dr. Jonas Salk announced on a radio show that he had a vaccine for polio and that the tests for the vaccine, so far, had been successful. He continued to test the

Table 4.2 Class Discussion Rubric

Below Expectations	**Approaching Expectations**	**Meets Expectations**	**Exceed Expectations**
Student does not participate in the discussion. Student does not listen to his peers.	Student listens intently and acknowledges peers but struggles to add to the discussion. Work on developing some ideas to share first and take courage in communicating your good, valid thoughts.	Student participates in the discussion offering ideas, thoughts, and opinions. Student listens to others. Student supports opinions with reasons.	Student participates in the class discussion offering ideas, thoughts, and opinions, and feelings. Student works hard to effectively communicate. Student listens and validates the opinions of others. Student supports opinions with reasons or examples. Student supports facts with evidence. Student remains focused and addressed the discussion questions when prompted.

vaccine and proceeded with clinical trials where thousands of school children participated (Blume & Geesink, 2000).

On April 12, 1955, Jonas Salk announced that the vaccine for polio that he had been testing was safe and effective. In that year, there were over 29,000 cases of polio; two years later, after wide distribution of the vaccine across America, the case number had decreased to only 6,000. Mothers and fathers around the world breathed a sigh of relief. The polio vaccine was embraced by humanity and widely distributed around the world. See the 1958 Press Release from President Eisenhower for details (Figure 4.2).

Who was Dr. Jonas Salk?

Dr. Jonas Salk is the scientist who developed a polio vaccine using new medical technology. He was born in New York City in 1914. Prior to his work on polio, he contributed to vaccine development for influenza during WWII. He cared deeply about serving humanity and using science to make large-scale change and improvements in the world around him. He was equipped and motivated to do what was necessary to find a solution to the polio problem.

Dr. Salk had the brilliant idea to use a new vaccine technology to create the vaccine. He was able to create an effective, preventative medicine for the poliovirus that was devastating the lives of children all over the world. After large-scale testing on willing volunteers, including himself and his children, he found that his vaccine would work!

Although Dr. Jonas Salk never won the Nobel Prize, his contributions to humanity cannot be denied. He was recognized by the President of the United States, Dwight D. Eisenhower, for his efforts in a press release published on April 22, 1955. In this document, released by the press secretary, James C. Hagerty, the work of Dr. Salk was commended (Figure 4.3). It said:

> The work of Dr. Salk is the highest tradition of selfless and dedicated medical research. By helping scientists in other countries with technical information; by offering to them the strains of seed virus and professional aid so that production of vaccine can be started by them everywhere, by welcoming them to his laboratory so that they may gain fuller knowledge, Dr. Salk is a benefactor of mankind.
>
> (Press Release, 1958)

Explore Activity: Journal Writing Prompt #1

Dr. Salk often asked the question, "Are we being good ancestors?" In the 1955 press release from Dr. Eisenhower to Dr. Salk, it said that "Dr. Salk was a benefactor of mankind." In your journal, reflect on the following: What is a benefactor of mankind? Do you think Dr. Salk was a benefactor of mankind? Do you think that he was a good ancestor? Why or why not? How can we be good ancestors? Support your opinions with reasons (Table 4.3).

Explain

Vaccines are medicines that help the body's immune response to diseases. When your immune system receives a vaccine for a particular disease, your immune system prepares a response to that disease. Therefore, if you ever are exposed to the disease later in life, you will not get the disease. Your body will be prepared. Your immune system will already have

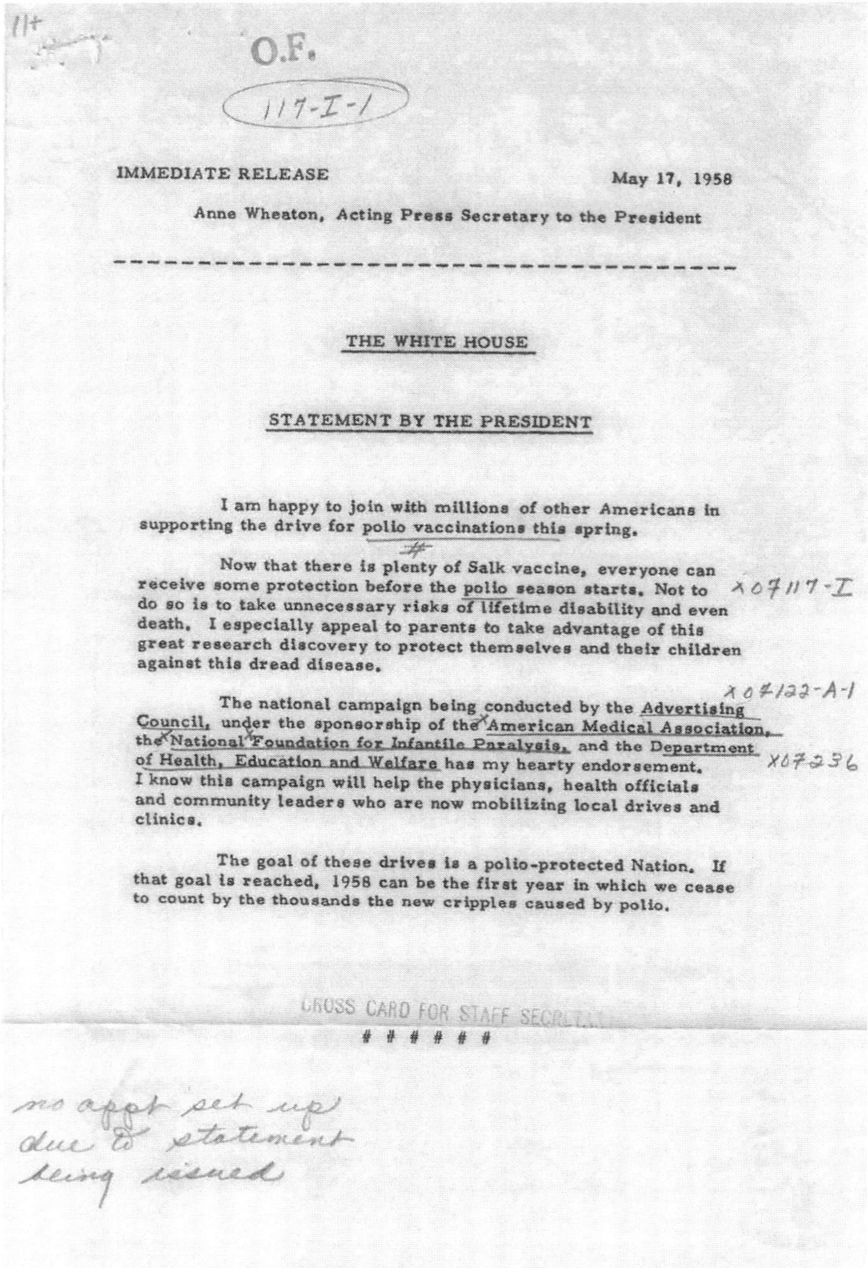

O.F.

117-I-1

IMMEDIATE RELEASE May 17, 1958

Anne Wheaton, Acting Press Secretary to the President

THE WHITE HOUSE

STATEMENT BY THE PRESIDENT

I am happy to join with millions of other Americans in supporting the drive for polio vaccinations this spring.

Now that there is plenty of Salk vaccine, everyone can receive some protection before the polio season starts. Not to do so is to take unnecessary risks of lifetime disability and even death. I especially appeal to parents to take advantage of this great research discovery to protect themselves and their children against this dread disease. X07117-I

X07122-A-1

The national campaign being conducted by the Advertising Council, under the sponsorship of the American Medical Association, the National Foundation for Infantile Paralysis, and the Department of Health, Education and Welfare has my hearty endorsement. X07236 I know this campaign will help the physicians, health officials and community leaders who are now mobilizing local drives and clinics.

The goal of these drives is a polio-protected Nation. If that goal is reached, 1958 can be the first year in which we cease to count by the thousands the new cripples caused by polio.

CROSS CARD FOR STAFF SECRET...

# # # # # #

no appt set up due to statement being issued

Figure 4.2 Press Release from President Eisenhower Supporting the Drive for Vaccinations (1958).

IMMEDIATE RELEASE April 22, 1955

James C. Hagerty, Press Secretary to the President

THE WHITE HOUSE

Following are the Citations given today by
the President to Dr. Jonas E. Salk and the
National Foundation for Infantile Paralysis

The Citation for Dr. Salk is as follows:

Because of a signal and historic contribution to human welfare by
Dr. Jonas E. Salk in his development of a vaccine to prevent
paralytic poliomyelitis, I, Dwight D. Eisenhower, President of
the United States, on behalf of the people of the United States,
present to him this citation for his extraordinary achievement.

The work of Dr. Salk is in the highest tradition of selfless and
dedicated medical research. He has provided a means for the
control of a dread disease. By helping scientists in other
countries with technical information; by offering to them the strains
of seed virus and professional aid so that the production of vaccine
can be started by them everywhere; by welcoming them to his
laboratory that they may gain a fuller knowledge, Dr. Salk is a
benefactor of mankind.

His achievement, a credit to our entire scientific community,
does honor to all the people of the United States.

The Citation for the National Foundation for Infantile Paralysis is as follows:

I, Dwight D. Eisenhower, President of the United States, present
this special citation to the National Foundation for Infantile
Paralysis for its unswerving devotion to the eradication of poliomyelitis.

The American people recognize a debt of gratitude to the Foundation
and to its founder, the late President Franklin D. Roosevelt, whose
personal courage in overcoming the handicap of poliomyelitis stands
as a symbol of the fight against this disease.

Without the support and encouragement of the Foundation, the work
of Dr. Jonas E. Salk and of many others who contributed to the
development of a preventive vaccine could not have gone forward so
rapidly. The Foundation displayed remarkable faith in sponsoring
and determination in fostering their valiant effort for the health of
all mankind.

The generous voluntary support of the Foundation by the American
people has been dramatically justified. In their name, I am privileged
to make this award to the National Foundation for Infantile Paralysis.

# # # # # # # #

Figure 4.3 Press Release Commending Dr. Jonas Salk for His Selfless Contributions to Science and Mankind.

Table 4.3 Rubric for Reflective Journal Writing

Below Expectations	**Approaching Expectations**	**Meets Expectations**	**Exceed Expectations**
Student does not respond to the journal prompt in writing or student writes a response, but the ideas are incoherent and not supported with reasons.	Student responds to some of the prompt in writing. Student shares opinions that are not supported with reasons or facts. Work on finding reasons and evidence to make stronger arguments in your written work.	Student responds to the journal prompt in writing. Student organizes their response in paragraphs. Student supports opinions with reasons or examples.	Student responds to the journal prompt in writing. Student organizes their response in paragraphs. Student supports opinions with reasons or examples. Student supports facts with evidence. Student communicates ideas thoughtfully and effectively.

the antibodies needed to fight any possible infection (Reece et al., 2014). When the polio vaccine was introduced, the rates of the virus decreased quickly in populations that were able to take the vaccine.

Key terms: poliomyelitis, virus, vaccine, immune response, antibodies

Dr. Salk, the scientist who first developed a safe and effective vaccine against the virus, used the scientific method to develop and test his solution to the real-world problem of the poliovirus. The results were amazing. Dr. Salk introduced new vaccine technologies when he hypothesized that we could use killed versions of the virus to produce an effective immune response. We would no longer have to use live/weakened viruses in all vaccines. This was a wonderful advancement in medical technology and has contributed to the development of many other vaccines since 1955.

Eventually, another vaccine using the weakened form of the virus proved to be effective as well. This second polio vaccine developed by Dr. Albert Sabine was cheaper and easier to distribute. It was distributed orally. Many children received the vaccine at school in a sugar cube that was placed gently on their tongue by the school nurse or community volunteers, usually mothers of the schoolchildren.

Making Decisions Based on Data

Part of using the scientific method and being scientifically literate is the ability to analyze data and make decisions based on that data. Some of the important data that was considered after the development of the polio vaccine is found in graphics called dot distribution or density distribution maps. Look at the distribution maps and answer the questions that follow. Draw some conclusions about the polio vaccine using the data found in the maps as evidence (Figures 4.4 and 4.5).

Technology and Society 91

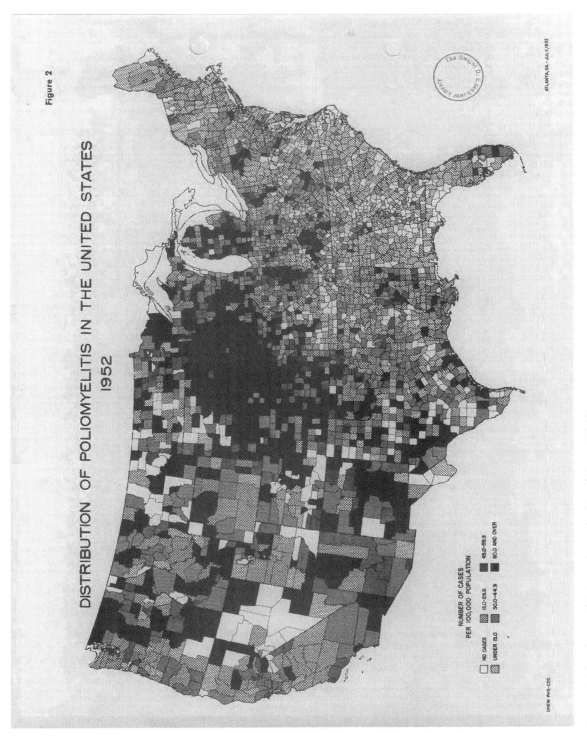

Figure 4.4 Distribution of Poliomyelitis in the United States (1952).

92   Technology and Society

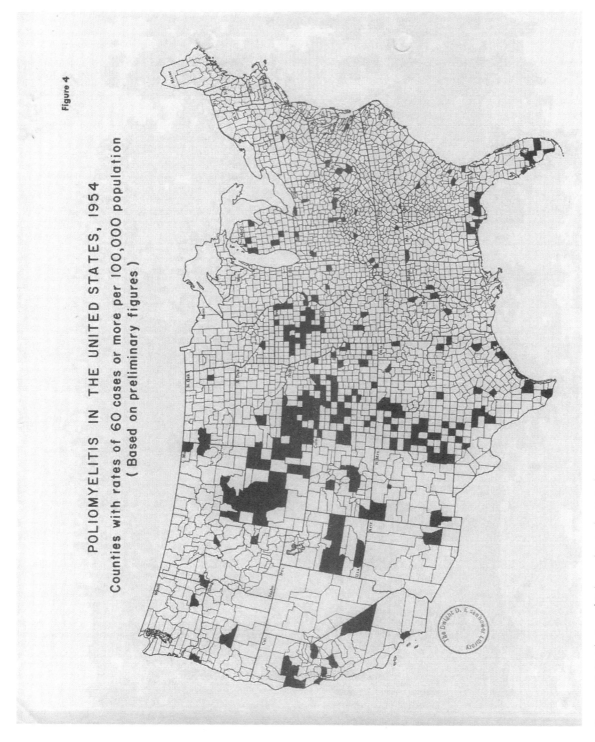

Figure 4.5 Distribution of Poliomyelitis in the United States (1954).

Technology and Society   93

Explain Activity

Look at the maps of the distribution of the poliomyelitis vaccine in 1952 and 1954. Analyze each map. Discuss with your small group.

1. What do you observe when you look at the maps? When was polio at its peak in the USA? What states were hit the hardest?
2. Compare and contrast the distribution of polio in 1952 and 1954. What factors might have contributed to the decreasing number of cases?
3. What would a map of the distribution of polio in the USA look like today? Why?

Elaborate

The development of a vaccine was not the only legacy and good news that came from the polio era. Another wonderful organization originated because of this terrible disease. The March of Dimes (https://www.marchofdimes.org/) was born during the time of polio and has bloomed into a source of care for babies, young children, and mothers. What started in a response to infantile paralysis, has become a lasting hope for supporting new families in America. The March of Dimes was started as the National Foundation for Infantile Paralysis on January 3, 1938 by President Franklin Delano Roosevelt (FDR), who had himself been personally affected when he contracted polio as a child and spent the remainder of his life in a wheelchair (Rose, 2010). The March of Dimes was instrumental in the development of the polio vaccine by raising awareness and funds.

Elaborate Activities

Today there are many ways that the March of Dimes helps children and their families. There are also several ways to volunteer and get involved in this work. Choose one of the following ways and start volunteering to help today:

1. **WonderWalk** – participate in the March of Dimes WonderWalk by raising funds. This is an event for preschool and elementary school children. Children can become a volunteer, and "learn about the mission of the March of Dimes and the value of helping others" (March of Dimes, 2020). Go here to learn more: https://www.marchofdimes.org/volunteers/get-involved-at-the-elementary-school-level.aspx
2. **Coin collection** – participate in fundraising for the March of Dimes by collecting coins. You can do this at home or in your classroom. Compete with other students to see who can collect the most coins and make the biggest difference in the lives of babies!

Evaluate

It is a miracle that the polio vaccine is nearly eradicated in the entire world. What was once a terrifying disease that preyed on children and babies has nearly disappeared. Why?

Because of Science!!!!

The people who lived through the polio outbreaks of the early 1900s waited with hope for a solution. Once the vaccine was available, they listened to the science, and they acted. Part of the success of widespread vaccine distribution was the fact that mothers wanted to protect their children. Many of them participated in the campaign for the vaccine by going door-to-door with the March of Dimes to raise awareness and provide information to other mothers who also wanted to protect their children.

"During the period when Jonas Salk developed the inactivated polio vaccine, or IPV, there was not much opposition to vaccines," says Dr. Walter A. Orenstein (2015), a professor of medicine, pediatrics, and global health at Emory University. Dr. Orenstein is also associate director of the Emory Vaccine Center. He says that people viewed the vaccine as a miracle.

Evaluate Activity: Journal Writing Prompt #2

Consider the consequences if people would not have been willing to take the polio vaccine. What would the world look like today? Imagine what the map of polio distribution in the United States might look like today if the polio vaccine had never been developed or utilized. Share your thoughts on this topic using reflective writing. Write about your feelings about the development of the polio vaccine and the worldwide outcomes of this medical technology. How important do you think medical technologies are for humanity? What are some possible positive or negative outcomes of medical technologies? Support your opinions with reasons or facts. See Table 4.3, the rubric for journal writing, to evaluate your work.

Project #8: Is YouTube Good For Me?
Academic Learning Objectives

Students will:

a) Read and analyze an international study on students' social media usage in the United States. Discuss the results of this study.
b) Investigate their own social media usage by collecting data on personal media use in a diary. Analyze and draw conclusions about the effects of social media on their health.
c) Create a graph using the data that they collected during their self-study. Explain the graph to a small group.
d) Write a reflection that answers the question: Is social media good for me? In the reflection, identify pros and cons of usage.
e) Write a set of rules for social media usage.

SEL Competencies

a) **Self-awareness:** Students will use honesty and integrity while conducting the self-study on social media use. They will honestly record their time spent doing different activities.
b) **Self-management:** Students will reflect on the need to manage their social media use and consider the role of self-discipline and motivation in behavior.
c) **Relationship skills:** Students will communicate effectively and clearly.

Essential Questions

1. How much time do I spend using social media?
2. How much time do people spend doing meaningful tasks on social media, such as:
   a. Connecting with other people / talking to friends / building relationships.
   b. Learning or doing homework.
   c. Being entertained.
3. Is the social media site YouTube good for me? How does it affect my health?
4. How can I manage the time that I spend doing on-screen versus off-screen activities?
5. How can social media support or constrain relationship building, making human connections, and learning?
6. What factors will motivate me to set healthy boundaries for social media consumption?

Stages of Inquiry

Introduction to the Problem

Social media has become a reality of everyday life for most Americans. We use various social media platforms to talk to friends, share information, learn, find jobs, find doctors, find help with our homework, play games, and many other things. One of the most popular social media sites today is YouTube. YouTube "is an online video sharing and social media platform" owned by Google. Around the world, its users watch more than one billion hours of YouTube videos each day. YouTube creators, popularly referred to as YouTubers, upload over 100 hours of content per minute. In 2005, Youtube.com was launched by Steve Chen, Chad Hurley, and Jawed Karim. (YouTube, 2021)

Did we read that correctly? One billion hours of YouTube video watching every single day? One hundred hours of new content uploaded per minute? That is a massive quantity of time and huge amounts of information. So, how can we know if this is a good use of our precious time? And how can we know if the information that we are accessing on YouTube is good, true, and reliable? Is YouTube good for us?

In this project, students will be asked to use an inquiry process to explore an important question: Is YouTube good for me? This project is a study of self-awareness and self-management when using social media. They will consider the pros and cons of YouTube and/or other social media website technologies. Students will evaluate the role that these social media sites can play in our lives through discussions and written reflections.

Engage

According to a study by Kaiser (2010), American kids aged 8 to 18 spend 7.5 hours a day in front of their screens. Much of this time is spent passively being entertained with activities such as watching TV. Other time is spent on social media sites, such as watching or commenting on videos on YouTube or TikTok, playing videogames, surfing the web, or engaging with friends online. This average does not include time spent engaging in academic tasks.

Engage Activity

Review the original report, "Generation M2: Media in the Lives of 8- to 18-Year-Olds" (2010) here: https://www.kff.org/wp-content/uploads/2013/01/8010.pdf

Read p. 1, the introduction to the study. With your class, jigsaw read the key findings, pp. 2–5.

In your small group, discuss the following (see Table 4.2 for the discussion rubric):

1. How many kids were included in the study?
2. What were the age ranges of the kids?
3. What are one or two of the key findings?
4. Which, if any, of the key findings surprised you?
5. This study was conducted in 2010. Do you think that the amount of media use by kids has changed since the conclusion of this study?

Explore

In the engage activities, you looked at a primary source document, a study of media use amongst 8–18-year old children. One method, or way that this group collected data for this study, was to ask students to complete a seven-day diary of their personal media use.

In this part of the project, you are going to use a similar methodology to understand your own media use. Keep a three-day diary of your media use (Table 4.4). Be honest about when, how much, and what kind of media you consume. Make sure that one day of data collection is on a weekend day (Saturday or Sunday) and the other two days are week days (Monday, Tuesday, Wednesday, Thursday, or Friday). In your diary, for each one-hour period of each day, you will answer the following two questions:

1. Did I use media during the hour?
2. During the hour, what did I do:
    a. Watch videos on social media such as YouTube or TikTok?
    b. Watch TV?
    c. Use the computer?
    d. Play videogames?

Table 4.4 Sample Diary Page

Name:					
Date:					
Day of the Week:					
Hour of the Day	Before 8:00am	8:00–9:00am	9:00–10:00am	10:00–11:00am	11:00–noon
Amount of time spent using media (Example: 15 minutes, 30 minutes, 45 minutes, 1 hour)					
Three main activities: (example: writing emails, watching YouTube, playing video games, etc.)					

Hour of the Day	Noon–1:00pm	1:00–2:00pm	2:00–3:00pm	3:00–4:00pm	4:00–5:00pm
Amount of time spent using media (example: 15 minutes, 30 minutes, 45 minutes, 1 hour)					
Three main activities: (example: writing emails, surfing the Internet, playing videogames, etc.)					

Hour of the Day	5:00–6:00pm	6:00–7:00pm	7:00–8:00pm	8:00–9:00pm	After 9:00pm
Amount of time spent using media (example: 15 minutes, 30 minutes, 45 minutes, 1 hour)					
Three main activities: (example: writing email, watching YouTube playing videogames, etc.)					

    e. Email, chat, or message with friends or family?
    f. Email teachers or turn in assignments online?
    g. Look at social media (read posts or watch videos posted by friends)?
    h. Respond to social media posts?
    i. Create media to post, such as taking pictures or making videos?
    j. Do homework?
    k. Read/research?
    l. Other _____?

Explore Activity

Once you have completed the three-day diary, analyze and reflect on your findings by answering the following questions:

1. How many hours per day on average did I spend using media?
2. What were the three main activities that I participated in the most?
3. Were you surprised by how much you used media during the day?
4. In your opinion, how did using this media benefit you? Which activities were beneficial? How?
5. In your opinion, did using this media harm you in any way? Which activities wasted your time?
6. In your opinion, what are some pros and cons of using media?

> **A Note to Teachers:** Please be mindful of students' individual access to media. If there is inequity in your classroom or lack of access to the Internet, you may modify this project to reflect your students' needs. For example, instead of recording individual media use, perhaps you can look at class averages or media use during the school day.

Explain

Now that you have data on how much media you use, create a visual display of this data. You may create a chart or a graph to represent how much media you use each day. Present your results to your class. Compare your results to your classmates. Compare your results to some of the results in the 2010 Kaiser study.

Elaborate

Now that we know how much time we spend consuming media, let us reflect on the pros and cons of those activities. Media technology and computer-based communication have many advantages. For example, consider how much easier and faster it is to send an instant message than to wait weeks for a mail delivery by the pony express. We can connect and stay in touch with friends and family no matter where in the world they are or what time of day it is! This is a wonderful advantage, connectiveness and communication. Unfortunately, this comes with some disadvantages. Just because we are always able to connect at any time of day or night, should we? Should we be expected to reply to text messages and emails any time day or night? When should we turn it off, take a break, and sleep?

Another advantage of digital media is that it keeps us informed about real-world events in real time. We can know what is going on around the world and can access news 24/7. Unfortunately, this constant bombardment of information can desensitize us, and leave us little time to process what we are learning about. How much is too much?

Another pro of social media is the ability to "take care of business" online. We can go to school online, do our banking online, and grocery shop online. It saves time and money in some cases. Of course, the issue of time can be a disadvantage too. If we spend too much time on social media, we might be missing out on doing other "real-world activities" that keep us healthy and interesting. You cannot play soccer, go swimming, or hike on a trail when you are staring at your computer screen.

Social media is a great place to share the wonderful things happening in your life with friends and family. You can post pictures and share adventures. The downside of this aspect of social media is that people may only share the good parts of their lives. They may be presenting a false perception of who they are. Others, who look at everyone's perfectly happy lives, may feel inadequate. Social media can negatively affect the self-esteem of children and adults alike. It is important to know who you are and to be confident in your abilities and real-life circumstances. Psychologists suggest that taking a break from social media at times can help teenagers stay connected to their real selves and not get caught up with false expectations for reality (Graham et al., 2020).

Another advantage of social media is that good people use it to do good things, such as help one another during a quarantine (see Project #4) or raise funds for healthy babies (see Project #7). Unfortunately, the opposite is also true. There are people using social media for bad purposes. Students must be careful and follow the rules and guidelines set by their parents and teachers to stay safe while using social media.

> **A Word of Caution:** Exercise good judgment about what information you share on social media. The digital information that you put out in the world can never be completely deleted! Therefore, be careful about what you post, and always act with integrity.

Elaborate Activity: Journal Prompt #3

Reflect in writing on the question: Is YouTube good for me? In your response, take a position and support your opinion with examples, data from your self-study, or facts. Discuss ways that you can exercise self-discipline to manage your social media use. See Table 4.3, Rubric for Journal Writing, to ensure that you include the required elements in your writing.

Evaluate

Now that we understand some of the pros and cons of social media use, perhaps it is time to set some rules for use. We have rules for everything, right? You have classroom rules, school rules, rules for sports, and rules at home. Rules are important because they help people know what to do. They also can help keep people safe and help kids develop morals, social skills, and healthy habits. Most schools have rules for using technology appropriately, fairly, and safely.

Evaluation Activity

Work with your small group to read the list in Table 4.5, School Rules for Using Technology. For each rule, write a justification. A justification is a reason that the rule is necessary. Some examples of justifications for rules include: This rule will keep me safe. This rule will help us be fair. This rule will help us do the right thing. This rule is important because it will keep our classroom clean and the technology working in good condition.

Discuss: What other rules would you add to this list that are important for school technology use?

Extension Activity

Some families have rules for social media and screen time use as well. Brainstorm three to five rules for using technology at home. For each rule, justify the reasons why this rule might be necessary. Make sure to include one rule about screen time limits.

A Note to Teachers: When considering using technology for school purposes, the U.S. Department of Education has given four guidelines for consideration (Policy Brief, 2016):

1. Technology can be a tool for learning. It should not be an add-on, something that students experience separate from academic learning opportunities, but rather as an integrated tool.
2. Technology should be used to increase access to learning for *all* children. We know that there still exists a digital divide between children of different socioeconomic backgrounds. It is the role of educators to ensure that they are using technology equitably.
3. Technology supports learning best when students and adults use it together, especially for young learners.
4. Technology is a wonderful tool for increasing the lines of communication between schools, teachers, families, and students, when used appropriately and creatively.

Table 4.5 School Rules for Using Technology

School Rule for Using Technology	Justification
1. Only visit approved websites. 2. Do not give out any personal information, including your name, address, phone number, school name, pictures, etc. 3. Do not eat or drink near devices. 4. Return devices to appropriate storage bins and connect them to chargers when you are finished using them. 5. Do not download anything or print anything without permission from your teacher. 6. Never chat online with a stranger. Tell your teacher if anything seems inappropriate.	

Project #9: Technology for Adventures

Academic Learning Objectives

Students will:

a) Work in small groups to brainstorm ideas about adventures. They will record benefits, possible locations, and necessary technologies for adventure in their geographic region.
b) Research a famous adventurer from history. Write a narrative from the perspective of the individual and present your story to the class.
c) Evaluate the importance of planning, finding resources, and preparing before going on an adventure. Use reflective writing to share a dream of an adventure that you want to take. Reflect on what it will take to make your dreams a reality.

SEL Competencies

a) **Self-awareness:** As students set goals and achieve goals, they will develop greater understanding about their interests and sense of purpose.
b) **Responsible decision-making:** Students will select appropriate and healthy goals and determine what resources are needed. They will begin to see how consequences of planning or lack thereof affect outcomes and goal attainment.
c) **Relationship skills:** Students will practice communicating using oral and written language when they work together to brainstorm ideas and share dreams about adventuring.

Essential Questions

1. Define the term adventure. What are some of the benefits of outdoor adventuring for our health?
2. What is the relationship between technology and adventure?
3. How important is planning, finding resources, and preparing, before going on an adventure?

Stages of Inquiry

Introduction to the Problem

The tallest mountain in the world is Mount Everest, located in the Himalayas. The most recent measurement of the height, including the snow on top, is 8,848.86 meters (Mount Everest, 2021). Many modern-day explorers dream of climbing to the top, and some do Humans have always craved outdoor adventure. Whether attempting to fly a rocket into space for a moonwalk, dive deep into the ocean, or scale the highest mountain peaks, humans throughout history have longed to conquer any remaining frontiers known on earth. To achieve most of these audacious dreams, humans have worked to utilize the most up-to-date technology available that will support them in the task. If the technology that they needed did not exist, humans worked to invent it, constantly developing new and better technologies used to quench the human thirst for adventure.

Many of the adventures occur in the great outdoors. In 2020, we saw an increase in participation in outdoor activities in nature (Outdoor Foundation Report, 2020). In fact, according to the Outdoor Foundations 2020 trend report, 7.1 million more Americans got outside for an outing than the year before. This was one remarkably positive result of the global pandemic that year. Outdoor adventures seemed to be a haven, improving emotional states and circumstances, for many people in America and around the world.

There are wonderful psychological and emotional benefits of adventuring. Piff et al. (2015) studied the "benefits of the awe," that feeling of amazement, joy, and appreciation that one experiences when seeking adventures. Experiencing awe is effective in improving emotional states. When we feel awe, we realize that we are only a small part of the enormous world. This perspective helps people exhibit more compassion, greater generosity, and increased ethical decision-making. The conclusion: Spending time on outdoor adventures increases your social-emotional competence and makes you a better person!

Beyond positive social behaviors, adventuring with others can improve communication skills and group decision-making skills. Teams who work together while exploring learn how to improve relationships and gain personal and social awareness. There are so many advantages to outdoor adventuring beyond the obvious benefits of improved physical health. Adventuring can also improve your mental health by reducing depression (Callister et al., 2013). These findings almost make you want to go on a hike right now, don't they?

Engage

Imagine going on a hike and getting lost. You have some technology in your backpack that will help you find your way. You pull out a map (technology) and a compass (technology), and with your supreme navigational skills, you work your way back on track and eventually reach your destination. It is in instances like this where you learn coping mechanisms for dealing with the uncertainties of life. Adventuring is good for this and many more reasons.

Engage Activity: Small Group Brainstorming Activity

a) First, brainstorm a list of ten reasons to go on an outdoor adventure.
b) Next, brainstorm a list of three possible places to adventure in your community. This could be a local park or hiking trail, a pond, or even a community garden found on the grounds of your school campus. There are so many places to explore if you start to look around.
c) Select one of the places that you discussed and determine three essential technologies to bring along with you when you go. These could include anything, like binoculars, a compass or GPS unit, a lantern or flashlight, some bug spray, or even a raincoat. All of these items are technologies that were developed so that

humans could thrive in outdoor spaces and places. These items are technologies used for adventures.

d) Finally, envision your group an adventure together. Draw a picture of what it will look like. In your picture, include the technologies that you chose as essential. Label them. Write a caption for your picture describing where you are and one of the benefits that you are receiving as a result of being there.

Example caption: This is me in the park using my binoculars to count the different species of birds. I am feeling peaceful and calm.

Explore

The benefits of adventuring would come as no surprise to some of the pioneers in exploration. In this project, we will investigate the accomplishments of a few heroic adventurers. We will consider their bravery, contributions to science, and stand in awe of places they traveled, sometimes being the first to step foot where they stepped. The superhuman feats you will read about may astound you, and you may begin to wonder how they were achieved and what helped the adventurers along the way! In every single one of the cases, the adventurers used the innovative technology of their day to get where they wanted to go. This technology can include anything from the lightweight but super-warm clothing that kept them alive in the subzero temperatures of the mountains to the supersonic speed rockets that catapulted them into orbit. Technology is application of scientific knowledge for practical purposes as well as any equipment or machinery developed from the application of science (Technology, 2021).

Explore Activity

Select an individual from the list in Table 4.6, or another famous explorer of the land, sky, or sea. Discover who they are, what they did and when, where they traveled, what technology they used, and what contributions they made to humanity.

Table 4.6 A List of Adventurers

A List of Adventurers
• Sylvia Earle, deep-sea explorer
• Amelia Earhart, pilot
• Lynn Hill, mountain explorer
• Edmund Hillary, mountain explorer
• Mae Jemison, astronaut
• Robert Lawrence, astronaut
• Norgay, Tenzing, mountain explorer
• Ellen Ochoa, astronaut
• Sally Ride, astronaut
• Junko Tabei, mountain explorer
• Weihenmayer Erik, mountain explorer
• Jacques-Yves Cousteau, deep-sea explorer

Explain

What can we learn from the adventurous spirits who have gone before us? In the explore phase of this project, you selected an individual and researched their accomplishments and their contributions to humanity. In this phase of inquiry, you will explain to the class what your explorer did, from their perspective.

Explain Activity: Write a Narrative

First, you will write a narrative from the point of view of the explorer that you researched. In the narrative, write the story about one of their adventures. Use the first person when you write. For example, if you selected Lynn Hill, your story might begin like this,

> Hello, my name is Lynn Hill and I am the first person, not the first woman, the first person, to ever free-climb the nose of El Capitan in Yosemite National Park. I'll never forget that day. I woke up before the sun came up, stretched, and put on my climbing shoes and harness. When I looked at the mountain in front of me, I was in AWE!

Extension Activity

Students present their narratives to the class using a dramatic, interpretive reading style. Consider allowing the students to wear a costume or bring props that would represent the individual and celebrate their achievements.

Elaborate

Amelia Earhart was the first woman to make a transatlantic flight. She believed that adventure for the sake of adventure was worth it. She believed that the process is the reward, even if success isn't achieved (The Family of Amelia Earhart, 2021). During the time of her transatlantic flight, Amelia Earhart was a pioneer of the air. She was a trailblazer for both female and male pilots who would follow in her adventurous footsteps (Figure 4.6).

Small Group Discussion Questions

1. What do you think of Amelia Earhart's ideas about adventure? Do you think that the process of trying to do something is worth it, even if you don't succeed?
2. Is adventure for the sake of adventure worth anything?
3. What are some of the benefits of going on adventures?

When you go on adventures in nature, you may become more conscious of protecting our environment and the plants and animals with whom we share the earth. You may become more aware of yourself and gain confidence in your abilities to try something new. Even if you don't make it to the top of the mountain, simply by beginning the climb you may discover that you aren't as afraid of heights as you thought. Perhaps Ms. Earhart was right, after all.

Figure 4.6 Amelia Earhart Standing by Her Airplane (1936).

Evaluate

Adventures require planning, resources, and preparation before they begin. In fact, most worthwhile things in life do too. But, adventures, like other accomplishments, usually start with a dream. The decision to climb Mount Everest or become an astronaut is only the first step in the long process toward realizing a dream. But, we have to dream. Dreaming is part of being a healthy individual. Dream first. Dreams can become goals, and goals are achievable if we plan, gather resources, use technology, prepare, and begin!

Evaluate Activity – Journal Prompt #4

What adventures do you dream about going on? Are they expeditions into the wild, or academic pursuits that will lead you toward your dream job? In this final reflective writing activity, list and describe one special adventure that you hope to take in your lifetime. Reflect on what it will take to get there. Write about the planning, resources, technology, and preparation that you will need to achieve your goal. Writing it down is the first step on the journey to making your dream come true.

Bibliography

Amelia Earhart; 7/30/1936; Records of the Army Air Forces, Record Group 18. [Online Version. Retrieved from https://www.docsteach.org/documents/document/amelia-earhart, August 1, 2021]

Altman, L.K. (1982, Aug. 3). Polio: A Painful Memory is Fading. The Doctor's World. *New York Times*. Archived Article. Retrieved on August 21, 2021 from https://www.nytimes.com/1982/08/03/science/the-doctor-s-world.html.

Ashbrook, P. (2020). Becoming Scientifically Literate. *Science and Children*, April/May 2020, 57(8). Retrieved on April 4, 2021 from https://www.nsta.org/science-and-children/science-and-children-aprilmay-2020/becoming-scientifically-literate.

Callister, R., Giles, A., Nasstasia, Y., Baker, A.L., Dascombe, B., Halpin, S., Hides, L., & Kelly B. (2013). Healthy Body Healthy Mind: Trialling an Exercise Intervention for Reducing Depression in Youth with Major Depressive Disorder. *International Journal of Exercise Science: Conference Proceedings*, 10(1), Article 6, 444–460. Retrieved on August 1, 2021 from https://digitalcommons.wku.edu/ijesab/vol10/iss1/6

Crichton, M. (2003, Jan. 17). Aliens Cause Global Warming. Caltech Micheline [lecture] transcript. Retrieved on April 4, 2021 from http://www.sepp.org/NewSEPP/GW-Aliens-Crichton.htm Caltech Michelin Lecture January 17, 2003

Distribution of Polio in the United States, 1952; 5/1955; Salk Vaccine - April and May 1955; Personal Files, 1929 - 1960; Collection DDE-1243: Oveta Culp Hobby Papers. [Online version, https://www.docsteach.org/documents/document/distribution-of-polio-in-the-united-states-1952, August 1, 2021].

Graham, S., Mason, A., Riordan, B., Winter, T., & Scarf, D. (2020). *Cyberpsychology, Behavior, and Social Networking*. 421–425.http://doi.org/10.1089/cyber.2020.0217

Kaiser Family Study. (2010). Generation M2: Media in the Lives of 8–18 Year Olds [report]. Retrieved on August 1, 2021 from https://www.kff.org/wp-content/uploads/2013/01/8010.pdf.

March of Dimes. (2021). Get Involved at the Elementary School Level. [webpage]. Retrieved on July 1, 2021 from https://www.marchofdimes.org/volunteers/get-involved-at-the-elementary-school-level.aspx

McCullers, J.A., & Dunn, J.D. (2008). Advances in Vaccine Technology and Their Impact on Managed Care. *P & T: A Peer-reviewed Journal for Formulary Management*, 33(1), 35–41.

Mount Everest. (2021). In Wikipedia. Retrieved on October 25, 2021 from https://en.wikipedia.org/wiki/Mount_Everest

National Governors Association Center for Best Practices, Council of Chief State School Officers. (2010). *Common Core State Standards (Insert Specific Content Area If You Are Using Only One)*. Washington D.C.: Author. Retrieved on August 1, 2021 from http://corestandards.org/

NGSS Lead States. (2013). Next Generation Science Standards: For States, by States. Retrieved on August 1, 2021 from http://www.nextgenscience.org

Orenstein, W.A. (2015). Defeating Polio, The Disease That Paralyzed America: NPR History Dept.: NPR [radio broadcast]. Retrieved on August 1, 2021 from https://www.npr.org/sections/npr-history-dept/2015/04/10/398515228/defeating-the-disease-that-paralyzed-america

Outdoor Foundation. (2020). *2020 Outdoor Participation Report*. Outdoor Industry Association. Retrieved on August 1, 2021 from https://outdoorindustry.org/resource/2020-outdoor-participation-report/

Paul, J.R. (1971). *A History of Polio Myelitis*. Yale University Press.

Piff, P.K., Dietze, P., Feinberg, M., Stancato, D.M., Keltner, D. (2015). Awe, The Small Self, and Prosocial Behavior. *Journal of Personality and Social Psychology*, Jun; 108(6):883–99. http://doi.org/10.1037/pspi0000018. PMID: 25984788.

Photograph of Nurses Being Instructed on the Use of Respirator for a Polio Patient; 5/23/1958; General Records of the Department of Labor, Record Group 174. [Online version https://www.docsteach.org/documents/document/photograph-of-nurses-being-instructed-on-the-use-of-respirator-for-a-polio-patient, August 1, 2021]

Polio Global Eradication Initiative (2021). History of Polio. [website] Retrieved on February 10, 2021 from https://polioeradication.org/polio-today/history-of-polio/

Polio in the United States, 1954; 5/1955; Salk Vaccine – April and May 1955; Personal Files, 1929 – 1960; Collection DDE-1243: Oveta Culp Hobby Papers. [Online version https://www.docsteach.org/documents/document/polio-in-the-united-states-1954, August 1, 2021]

Press Release. (1958). Statement by the President Supporting the Drive for Polio Vaccinations; 5/17/1958; OF 117-I-1 Salk Polio Vaccine (10); Official Files, 1953–1961; Collection DDE-WHCF: White House Central Files (Eisenhower Administration); Dwight D. Eisenhower Library, Abilene, KS. [Online version https://www.docsteach.org/documents/document/press-release-president-supporting-polio-vaccinations, August 1, 2021].

Reece, J.B., Urry, L.A., Cain, M.L., Wasserman, S.A., Minorsky, P.V., Jackson, & Campbell, N.A. (2014). *Campbell Biology* (10th edition). Boston, MA: Pearson.

Remarks by Oveta Culp Hobby, Secretary of Health, Education, and Welfare, Given at a Conference on the Salk Polio Vaccine; 4/22/1955; OF 117-I–1 Salk Polio Vaccine (6); Official Files, 1953 - 1961; Collection DDE-WHCF: White House Central Files (Eisenhower Administration); Dwight D. Eisenhower Library, Abilene, KS. [Online version https://www.docsteach.org/documents/document/remarks-secretary-of-health-education-and-welfare-salk-polio-vaccine, August 1, 2021].

Rose, D. (2010). A History of the March of Dimes. The Polio Years. [March of Dimes website archives] Retrieved on July 15, 2021 from https://www.marchofdimes.org/mission/a-history-of-the-march-of-dimes.aspx

Smithsonian National Museum of American History. *Whatever Happened to Polio?* [online]. Retrieved on December 18, 2018 from http://americanhistory.si.edu/polio/

Blume, S. & Geesink, I. (2000, June). A Brief History of Polio Vaccines. *Essays of Science and Society*, 288(5471), 1593–1594.https://doi.org/10.1126/science.288.5471.1593

Tan, S.Y., & Ponstein, N. (2019). Jonas Salk (1914–1995): A Vaccine Against Polio. *Singapore Medical Journal*, 60(1), 9–10. https://doi.org/10.11622/smedj.2019002

Technology. (2021) in Oxford Learner Dictionary. Retrieved on October 26, 2021 from https://www.oxfordlearnersdictionaries.com/us/definition/english/technology?q=technology

The College of Physicians of Philadelphia. (2021). Polio Notice. *The History of Vaccines*. Retrieved on April 8, 2021 from https://www.historyofvaccines.org/timeline/

The Family of Amelia Earhart. (2021). Quotes – The Official Licensing Website of Amelia Earhart [Website]. Retrieved on August 1, 2021 from http://www.ameliaearhart.com/quotes/

US Department of Education. (2016, October). Early Learning and Educational Technology Policy Brief [policy brief]. Retrieved on July 1, 2021 from https://tech.ed.gov/files/2016/10/Early-Learning-Tech-Policy-Brief.pdf.

White House Press Release With the Text of Citations Given by the President to Dr. Jonas E. Salk and the National Foundation for Infantile Paralysis; 4/22/1955; OF 117-I–1 Salk

Polio Vaccine (8); Official Files, 1953–1961; Collection DDE-WHCF: White House Central Files (Eisenhower Administration); Dwight D. Eisenhower Library, Abilene, KS. [Online version https://www.docsteach.org/documents/document/white-house-press-release-about-dr-jonas-e-salk, August 1, 2021].

YouTube. (2021, June 1). In Wikipedia. Retrieved on June 1, 2021 from https://en.wikipedia.org/wiki/YouTube